Praise for *Co*

"Scott Ritter is an American treasure. No one on this side of the Atlantic has articulated a clearer or more thorough understanding of Russian history and culture. In this small book, he has put together a lucid and powerful attack on the Biden administration ignorance of all things Russian and consequent folly in Ukraine. Do yourself a favor and read it. Even though I know Scott well, I couldn't put this book down. On its pages you will see courage personified and the lessons of history made manifest."

HON. ANDREW P. NAPOLITANO, host of *Judging Freedom* podcast;
Senior Judicial Analyst for NewsMax

"Scott Ritter's voice has been essential for piercing through the lies behind the U.S.-NATO proxy war in Ukraine, and his regular conversations with Ania K are a critical example of both the information and transnational cooperation we need to get humanity closer to peace. This book provides key moments in their exchanges which are informative, accessible, and serve as an invaluable tool for anyone seeking the truth about one of the most consequential conflicts in modern history."

DANNY HAIPHONG, host of *The Left Lens with Danny Haiphong* podcast

"*Covering Ukraine: The Scott Ritter Interviews Through the Eyes Of Ania K* is a journey into the heart of a conflict that has reshaped the geopolitical landscape of the 21st century. This riveting account delves beyond headlines and statistics, offering a poignant exploration of the human experiences and strategic maneuvers that define this ongoing struggle. Through meticulously researched narratives and exclusive interviews, the book unveils the raw truths behind the war—highlighting NATO's delusional attitude and its consequences for Ukraine. *Covering Ukraine: The Scott Ritter Interviews Through the Eyes Of Ania K* is an essential read for anyone seeking to understand the complexities and stakes of this pivotal global crisis."

NIMA ROSTAMI ALKHORSHID, host, *Dialogue Works*

"Whether you read this book straight through, take in the interviews one at a time, or search it for a specific topic or subject, you will have furthered your understanding of the past, present and future of the war in Ukraine. There is no greater American authority on this war, the Russian military and the American Empire than Scott Ritter, and this book's interview style makes that apparent. This is a necessary book full of thought and insight into war and geopolitics. Scott and Ania's conversations delve into the deeper, psychological reasons for what we see occurring in terms of individuals, nations and history, making this book invaluable"

MATTHEW HOH, former U.S. Marine officer and diplomat; peace activist

More Praise for *Covering Ukraine*

"Covering Ukraine: The Scott Ritter Interviews Through the Eyes Of Ania K. is a brilliant piece that provides readers with a deep understanding of Russia's Special Military Operation through the experience and personal context of an experienced Western military intelligence professional. Those who have little or no military background will easily develop an emotional and spiritual bond with Ania and readily identify with her concerns about the dangers of an expanded conflict that can spiral out of control. I highly recommend this work and genuinely hope that it quickly spreads throughout the Western world."

GARLAND NIXON, host, *NewsViews with Garland Nixon*

COVERING UKRAINE
The Scott Ritter Interviews
Through the Eyes Of Ania K

Ania K
with
Scott Ritter

Foreword by Andrei Martyanov
Afterword by Larry Johnson

Clarity Press, Inc.

ISBN: 978-1-963892-08-6
EBOOK ISBN: 978-1-963892-09-3

In-house editor: Diana G. Collier
Typesetting design: Becky Luening

Library of Congress Control Number: 2024939432

Clarity Press, Inc.
2625 Piedmont Rd. NE, Ste. 56
Atlanta, GA 30324, USA
https://www.claritypress.com

Contents

Introduction

Ania K

I remember it as if it was yesterday—breaking news, February 24, 2022: "Putin has invaded Ukraine!"

At the very moment when I heard the news, I instinctively knew that something was off, that something was not presented to the masses in a way that reflected reality (what's new here).

At a time when the world was being turned upside down by this new geopolitical trauma, my own personal situation with my family was likewise in transition, and I was being called to return to my native Poland, compelled to leave the life I had made for myself in America behind.

What seemed like a series of unfair life adjustments at the time, however, were later revealed to me as part of God's master plan—I was taken to Poland because that was exactly where I needed to be in order to report on what was happening in the nation of my birth, whether it was the situation regarding refugees from Ukraine, the approach of Polish government to this new conflict, or the massive militarization of my motherland that was taking place in the name of NATO security.

As the Special Military Operation (Russia's name for what the West was calling the invasion of Ukraine) was unfolding, I wanted to connect with people who could help me to understand the reasons behind this action, what the intentions of Russia were in undertaking this traumatic step, and the geopolitical consequences of this military action. It was at that time that I came across Scott Ritter, the military expert, and a former United Nations weapons inspector.

I must admit to no small amount of nervousness as I prepared for my first interview with Scott, since I had never before interviewed a person possessing his experience with the very issues where his experience mattered most. There I was, a Polish woman without any military knowledge trying my best to be professional and to deliver to my audience the answers that we were all searching for.

Somehow, we found a way to not only make this interview work, but in doing so, create something that borders on the magical. Our online collaboration was initiated at that point, and now, two years on, Scott has been the most viewed guest on my YouTube channel ("Through the Eyes Of"). He is loved by millions of viewers around the world, if for no other reason than that he has a knack for explaining the most complicated matters on the military/geopolitical scene in words that a layperson can understand. Through this process, I've learned a lot from Scott, not just about the United States, but also about Russia.

And so has my audience.

But these interviews reveal so much more than just facts presented in an easy-to-understand manner. Over the course of these two years, I've asked hundreds of questions which elicit answers that I believe also showed the side of Scott which you hardly see on other channels—the heart and soul of the man.

I will forever be grateful for Scott Ritter's courage and commitment to the truth, and for honoring me by empowering me to have a role in telling it.

My intention for this book is to bring the following message to the world:

"Don't be afraid to ask questions. Seek the truth and, when you find it, be brave enough to stand alongside and proclaim it as loudly as possible, because when you are empowered by the truth, it is not the time to be a coward in the face of those who promulgate lies."

I believe that Scott and I have a mission to build the bridges between the nations and to show the world that people of different nationalities, whether Polish and Russian, American and Russian, or any other nation and Russian, can be friends capable of collaborating and respecting one another and, most importantly, who can create the conditions for peace instead of war.

Lots of love to everyone. We are the leading edge of a movement that will save humanity.

Ania K
Moscow, Russia

Follow Ania on YouTube.

Introduction

Scott Ritter

When the Russian Special Military Operation/invasion of Ukraine broke out, back on February 24, 2024, I was overwhelmed with requests for interviews from various media outlets, mainstream and alternative alike. It was a hectic time, and I would often find myself plugging in 12 or more hours a day sitting in front of a camera taking questions from people possessing a wide range of political beliefs and before audiences around the world.

I did my best to answer all queries I deemed to be legitimate but was always on guard for those which might be more interested in creating controversy than eliciting fact-based analysis. I recall receiving an email from Ania and wondering what the motivation could be of a lady from Poland in interviewing me, given the fact that Poland was a NATO member and a vociferous opponent of Russia's military operations in Ukraine. I took a gamble and agreed to an interview.

It turned out to be the right choice.

I first met Ania staring at her visage on a computer screen. In fact, it's the only way we have met—through the vehicle of the online interview. But I was captivated by her intelligence and humanity as they were manifested in the form of her questions, which probed not only the facts as they existed, but—perhaps most importantly—the reasoning behind these facts.

I was used to interviews that tested my mind. Ania's interviews tested my soul, and over the course of the next two years, I found myself both welcoming our time together, because Ania was always prepared with relevant questions, but also dreading it, because she always dug deeper into my emotions than any other interviewer. I would often finish an interview with Ania emotionally drained, a fact which, given the enormity of the subjects we covered, meant Ania was doing her job well.

I had been discussing with Diana Collier the possibility of an interview-based book on the war in Ukraine since the fall of 2022. The ever-changing nature of this conflict made the mechanism of the set-piece interview unwieldy, as the war being discussed in the interview would not be the war that existed at the time of publication.

Following the defeat of the Ukrainian 2023 summer counteroffensive, however, the Russian Special Military Operation has reached a stage where an outcome can now be predicted even if the specific timing of that outcome remains uncertain. The timing was conducive to an interview-based book, and, upon reflection, it was obvious who the interviewer should be—Ania K, the brave Polish lady who had challenged my brain and tortured my soul with her questions over the past two years.

This book is not only a history of the war in Ukraine, but more importantly, a journey of discovery as seen through the eyes of Ania and narrated by me, based upon her probing questions.

It is also a guide to how humanity should approach difficult issues, and I thank Ania for allowing me to be a part of it.

Scott Ritter
Delmar, New York

Follow Scott Ritter on Substack.

Foreword

Andrei Martyanov

If there ever was a better encapsulation of what any book is all about, it is by way of Ania K in the words of indomitable Scott Ritter: "I was used to interviews that tested my mind. Ania's interviews tested my soul, and over the course of the next two years, I found myself both welcoming our time together." So did I, having had many talks with both Ania and Scott. I count knowing them both as a privilege. This book is the best primer available on the market on the war in Ukraine, known in Russia as the Special Military Operation (SMO). These interviews are not by some corrupt legacy media journalist from the West "questioning" some anonymous (for some reason they are almost always anonymous) government bureaucrat or some washed out U.S. or NATO general who lost every war they ever fought. Rather, this book is by people who are competent both in human and military terms. And there is also no doubt about the human and professional integrity of Ania and Scott. Ania knows Russian culture very deeply, having been a frequent guest there and having many Russian contacts. So does Scott Ritter, a former U.S. Marine Corps intelligence officer and UN weapons inspector. Theirs is a combination of soul and knowledge which is crucial in providing a tether of truth about the events of the SMO to a Western public completely insulated from competent opinions and which is floating into the horrifying echo chamber of Western propaganda and outright lies.

Through his interviews with Ania and her poignant questions, Scott Ritter delivers a tour de force of strategic thinking and discloses facts which are either completely absent from Western legacy media or are being removed from public opinion, having been relegated to what could be defined as last pages of newspapers or to "small print." It is enough to point out Ritter's excellent elaborations on the back end of operations, including logistics and how complex it is for even a single brigade to move in combat zone. This book also serves as an excellent timetable of the SMO because Ania interviewed Scott for the last two years. Moreover, you can access those interviews on YouTube and see for yourself how people of integrity and humanity communicate with each other. I cannot recommend this book highly enough, especially because it is being published by what has become for Scott, Ania and me our intellectual home—Clarity Press.

Andrei Martyanov
Seattle, Washington

Follow Andrei on his blog.

NOTE

The interviews contained herein have been edited for grammar and clarity, without changing the substance. The original interview from which the text has been extracted can be found using the QR Code at the end of each chapter. The interviews contained in this book unfold in a rough chronological sequence that is broken on occasion to preserve the emotional gravity of the narrative, where the impact of what is being said was deemed by the authors as being more important than when it was said.

CHAPTER ONE

The Law of War

| February 23, 2023 |

The U.N. General Assembly votes 141 to 7, with 32 abstentions, to call for a lasting peace in Ukraine.

On the eve of the anniversary of the start of Russia's full-scale invasion of Ukraine, the United Nations General Assembly adopted a resolution calling for peace.

The United Nations General Assembly on Thursday adopted a resolution calling for a lasting peace in Ukraine and reiterating its demand for Russia to withdraw its troops and halt the conflict, in a nonbinding vote on the eve of the anniversary of Moscow's invasion.

The resolution, introduced by Ukraine during a special session of the assembly that lasted two days, passed 141 to 7, with 32 abstentions.

The resolution demonstrated continued support for Ukraine and Russia's isolation on the world stage even as many countries grapple with the far-reaching consequences of the war on their own populations, with the prices of energy and food soaring.

Among the countries that abstained were Russia's allies China, Iran and India. Among the few countries siding with Russia in voting no were Belarus, Eritrea, Nicaragua, North Korea, Mali and Syria. Two amendments offered by Belarus to alter the resolution in favor of Russia were rejected.

"In this war there is no equal sides; there is an aggressor and a victim," Ukraine's foreign minister, Dmytro Kuleba, told the assembly on Wednesday when he introduced the resolution. "We have no choice but to keep fighting for our survival."

Russia called the resolution "Russophobic," and its ambassador to the United Nations, Vassily Nebenzia, told the assembly on Wednesday that the idea of defeating "a nuclear state" was a fantasy.

Resolutions passed by the General Assembly are not legally binding, but they carry symbolic and political weight. This was the third one adopted by the assembly in relation to Russia's invasion of Ukraine a year ago. The Security Council has been unable to bring stronger action because Russia has veto power against any resolutions brought against it.

The United States and its European allies, who have stood staunchly with Ukraine and provided it with advanced military equipment and weapons to defend itself, view the adoptions of the three resolutions as a means to pressure Russia and showcase its isolation.

Farnaz Fassihi, *The New York Times,* February 23, 2023

Ania K: *There is something that I have been wondering about for quite some time. I believe if there is a war, every war has some kind of rules that cannot be crossed...you must respect those rules and you must stay within those rules, otherwise... there are consequences, right? Tribunals or courts or whatever it is. So, watching this situation in Ukraine, I'm wondering is there any kind of rule that has been respected in this situation, or are they breaking every single rule?*

Scott Ritter: Well...we can start with the beginning. Russia made a case to defend their decision to send military forces into Ukraine under article 51 of the United Nations Charter. Specifically, the case deals with preemptive collective self-defense. From the Russian perspective, they had a legal right and, indeed, they will say, Russia had duty and obligation to intervene militarily.

The collective West [NATO, the U.S., the European Union], including Ukraine, have rejected this. The United Nations has rejected this. But these are political decisions, not legal decisions. Let's just say that there's legal controversy here about the legality of Russia's actions.

But Russia's decision seems to be sustained more and more by the admission on the part of the collective West that they were in fact doing that which Russia accused them of doing, using a peace process [the Minsk Accords] as a sham to build up forces to attack Ukraine. We have video statements of President Zelensky in 2019 saying, "I will go to war in Ukraine, I will go to war in the Donbas!"

This is a time when the Minsk Accords were still on the table, and he [Zelensky] is acknowledging that he has no intention of fulfilling Minsk. And when you see that, Russia's case becomes stronger and stronger for a legal justification for their decision to intervene militarily.

A lot of people say that when you start a war based upon an illegal act, that's an illegal war of aggression, and everything that follows is by necessity illegal. So, it's important that we start at the beginning. Russia started this war based upon legitimate, legally sound, collective self-defense requirements that were brought about by eight years of NATO-assisted Western Ukrainian aggression against the people of the Donbas, together with clearly articulated intent on the part of NATO to use Ukraine as a military proxy to bring further harm to the people in Donbas and the people of Crimea and that rather than allowing this threat to manifest itself in action, Russia preempted it and moved in militarily.

If you look at Russia's goals and objectives early on, we now know that Russia wasn't trying to occupy Ukraine or destroy Ukraine; Russia was trying to compel Ukraine into a negotiated settlement. Russia invaded on February 24 [2022], and by March 2 they were already entering into negotiations—three negotiations in the first week of March and finally a concluding negotiation in Istanbul on April 1 that was supposed to bring this war to an end. Russia's actions conform with the case they made for intervention, namely the elimination of the immediacy of the threat to seek a peaceful resolution to the problem. Everything Russia has done has conformed with the letter and intent of the law.

Ukraine on the other hand was allowing itself to be used as a proxy by NATO to wage a genocidal war against the ethnic Russians. I call it genocidal because, you know, in April of 2014 Ukraine declared the ethnic Russian people of the Donbas and Crimea as terrorists, and they began an anti-terrorist operation that manifested itself in extreme violence, including stuffing 150 people into a trade Union building in Odessa, setting it on fire, and cheering as 48 of them died, the rape and pillaging of Mariupol in June of 2014, and the violence that ensued since then.

The crimes being committed by Ukraine are being backed by NATO and the collective West, who are empowering them with training and with political support—especially a coup d'etat [in February 2014] that was in violation of sovereign Ukrainian law, and in violation of the concept of self-determination.

So, when you do up a basic list of which side has the law on their side, fact-based, and not the knee-jerk, black-and-white stuff that the West wants you to buy into, where you have to assume at face value that Russia's actions were unprovoked active aggression . . . When you really look at it, you realize not only did Russia articulate a case [for intervention], but they've been acting in a manner which indicates that what they're seeking was indeed a rapid resolution of the war with minimal violence to achieve a peaceful outcome that was denied to them because of the other side's unwillingness to faithfully engage in negotiations.

We see that Russia is on the right side of history.

Now, look at what follows—how has Russia prosecuted this war? How has Ukraine prosecuted this war?

Russia has bent over backwards to avoid civilian loss of life. Tragically, thousands of Ukrainian civilians have lost their life in this conflict. But if you take a look at it, historically speaking, especially when we're dealing with large-scale grand combat operations in a European environment where you have dense populations—towns, villages etc.—that get caught up in the conflict, the civilian casualties roughly correlate to one to one. So to every dead soldier there is a dead civilian.

Let's look at a historical example: the American and French and British liberation of Normandy, and the battles that were fought there, in June and July 1944. Sixty thousand French civilians were killed, and yet we call it a just campaign, justifiable campaign—the liberation of France from the German occupier. Sixty thousand correlates to the total number of dead among the Germans and the Allies in that region.

In Ukraine today, a one-to-one correlation, where for every dead combatant one gets a dead civilian roughly…in the conflict to date Ukraine has probably suffered over 300,000 dead soldiers. The Russians have probably suffered between 35,000 and 40,000 dead soldiers. So we're looking at, say, 350,000 dead combatants. Therefore, there should be 350,000 dead civilians, using historical examples. Instead, the number of Ukrainian [civilian] dead is surprisingly low. We don't know the total numbers yet, but it is under 10,000, maybe just a little bit over 10,000, but it's not much larger than that.

So right off the bat we have a huge deviation between the number of civilian dead and the number of combatant dead. The historical precedent of one to one…it's far less than that. If you have 350,000 dead combatants, a one to ten ratio would make it 35,000 dead civilians. We have one third of that, so we're talking about a three percent casualty ratio instead of a one-to-one.

The numbers of [civilian] dead are surprisingly low. How did we get to this point? We know from Amnesty International, and we know from The Washington Post and others that the Ukrainians are using the Ukrainian civilians as human shields. Most of the Ukrainian civilians died because the Ukrainian government has put them in harm's way in violation of international humanitarian law, using them as human shields.

The Russians, on the other hand…we have some cases where the Russians have killed civilians; war is hell, and you get collateral damage, and you get things that you don't want…who knows, maybe some of those cases could manifest themselves into individual war crimes. But you can't sit there and say because you have an example of a Russian tank shooting on a civilian car killing an old man and a woman that Russia is prosecuting a war in violation of international humanitarian law because the evidence is completely different.

The Russians are going out of their way not to target civilian areas. It is very precise targeting, hitting critical infrastructure at a time designed to minimize human loss. When you do you lose people in those areas, it's because Ukrainian air defense has either missed the Russian missile and hit a building themselves or deflected a Russian missile into a building. But when Russia's bombs hit their targets, the targets are exclusively of military character with minimal civilian loss.

If you take a look at the fighting in urban areas such as Mariupol, we know that the Ukrainians, especially the neo-Zazis [the Azov Regiment], were holding hundreds of Ukrainian civilians hostage in buildings that they had occupied from a military standpoint, basically daring the Russians to destroy the building.

How did the Russians respond?

They didn't destroy the building. Instead, the Russians fought through the Ukrainian defenses, suffering large casualties to get to the civilians trapped in the building, to evacuate the civilians before launching the final attack on the building. This was repeated over and over and over again.

The Russians are not only complying with international humanitarian law—they are going above and beyond, because under humanitarian law they didn't have to do that. Once the Ukrainians turned that building into a military object which was impeding Russia's military objectives, then Russia had every right to apply the force necessary to eliminate that threat, and if the civilians die in the process that is collateral damage.

Instead, the Russians are going out of their way to avoid collateral damage. The Russians are sacrificing the lives of their soldiers to save human lives. The Russians are capturing Ukrainian prisoners of war and treating them well. Not just your average Ukrainian—they're capturing Nazis, people with swastikas, with the tattoos, people whose cell phones show them committing horrific crimes against civilians against Russian soldiers, and instead of executing them or torturing them, they [the Russians] bring them in and they treat them in accordance with international law. They provide them with shelter, food, medical care, and give them access to the International Red Cross. In many cases, they exchange them for Russian prisoners of War.

The Ukrainians, when they do capture Russians—we now know, through video evidence, that they execute a lot of Russians, they torture Russians, they do medical experimentation—castration—on Russian prisoners, they beat them, and when they release them, the Russians are in horrific mental state and physical state.

The bottom line is the Ukrainian government is waging the conflict in direct violation of every norm...they're executing prisoners—civilians. They [the Ukrainians] come in and they carry out cleansing operations where they grab civilians they accused of collaboration and execute them. You have Ukrainian military people bragging, saying that when the war is done, [the government] is going to "have to do a census to find out how many people we killed because we're killing them by the thousands, but we just dispose of the bodies."

Watch the full interview.

CHAPTER TWO

The Reality of War

| March 13, 2023 |

Heavy casualties reported in Bakhmut as battle for city rages.

Ukraine and Russia say thousands have been killed or badly wounded as each side battles for control of the town.

Ukraine and Russia have reported heavy casualties as the slow, grinding fight for control of the salt-mining town of Bakhmut continues in eastern Ukraine.

Ukraine controls the area to the west of the now ruined and nearly deserted Bakhmut, while Russia's Wagner Group controls most of the eastern part, according to British intelligence, with the Bakhmutka River that winds through the town marking the front line.

Ukraine's President Volodymyr Zelenskyy said more than 1,100 Russian soldiers had been killed in the past few days fighting along the Bakhmut section of the front line.

"In less than a week, starting from the 6th March, we managed to kill more than 1,100 enemy soldiers in the Bakhmut sector alone, Russia's irreversible loss, right there, near Bakhmut," Zelenskyy said in his nightly video address.

He added that some 1,500 Russian soldiers had been so badly wounded they were unable to continue fighting.

> *Russia's defense ministry said its forces were conducting further military operations in the eastern Donetsk region which, together with neighboring Luhansk, makes up the industrial Donbas.*
>
> *The ministry said Russian forces had killed more than 220 Ukrainian service members over the past 24 hours.*
>
> Reuters, March 13, 2023

Ania K: *Looking at how the Kiev regime is recruiting more troops, grabbing them from the streets and kidnapping them, I would like to know how that soldier who was taken off the streets can even deliver anything on the battlefield, with that much resentment towards the fight and the war?*

Scott Ritter: Well, here is what they are hoping for with that individual. First of all, they are not putting him in a unit compromised of people in a similar condition. I mean, if I kidnapped 100 guys, put them together, gave them guns, gave them ammunition and then said "go" and "die," they might turn their guns on me. Didn't anybody learn about Russian Revolution?

But you know what they do is, they take these guys and then they send them out to other units, basically to build them up. So you might, let's say, you have a squad of 10 guys, you're going to take 3 of these guys, put them in with 10 guys who are more or less committed to the fight, and then you put them into the situation where the hope is that the survival instinct will kick in. So, basically, it's hell on earth, and all they want you to do is to be a presence to make the assault on the Russians more difficult and they are more than happy if you die.

They don't care; what they're trying to do is to buy time for other units to be prepared, trained, organized, equipped, so that they can engage in some sort of counter-offensive down the road. So, these guys have just one job, to live a couple of days before dying.

Ania K: This is horrifying.

Scott Ritter: It is. It's the reality of war.

I mean, when one reflects back on the Battle of Stalingrad and in those desperate early weeks of the battle, in the late summer, early fall when the Russians were literally taking troops without enough guns and ammunition and throwing them across the river, and if you didn't have a gun you were told, wait until somebody gets hit who has a gun, then pick up his gun and go. And they just threw human waves after human waves to stop the Germans. That was the goal, to stop the Germans and then they were able to suck the Germans into the trap.

I don't know how this battle is going to end but I think I have a good idea, and it's with a Russian Victory. But you know this is an extraordinarily difficult fight under extraordinarily difficult circumstances, and the Ukrainians are desperate; they know, Zelensky has finally been honest enough to say it, "we lose Bakhmut, we lose the Donbas," that if Bakhmut falls then the Russians will be able to basically take Donbas. And so, they are pouring everything they have into this fight.

Watch the full interview.

CHAPTER THREE

Russia Is No Longer Looking for a Negotiated Settlement...

| April 14, 2022 |

The West must be prepared to discuss Ukraine's unconditional surrender.

Russian Ambassador to UN: Get ready to discuss Ukraine's surrender.

The West must be prepared for discussions of the unconditional surrender of Ukraine already in the near future, Russia's Ambassador to the UN Vasily Nebenzya said, TASS reports.

"Very soon, the only topic for any international meetings on Ukraine will be the unconditional surrender of the Kyiv regime. I advise you all to prepare for this in advance," Nebenzya said.

Andrey Mihayloff, *Pravda.ru*, April 11, 2024

Ania K: *The way I look at Ukraine, not being an expert, I see it this way: Putin wants to denazify Ukraine, he wants to liberate the ethnic Russian citizens that live in that region; I believe that he wants to rescue the children because there is a lot of human trafficking going on; he wants to take over the bio-labs and he also wants to show the Collective West that he is no longer going to put up with their behavior anymore, that means, back off NATO, back off whoever is there against Russia; I am at this point, as a country, strong enough to be sovereign, to get rid of* *those deals with the U.S. Petro-dollar and, to be free from sick systems, and not to be threatened anymore.*

That's how I perceive it from Putin's side.

Now, from the U.S./NATO/Europe, I see, first of all, there is corruption at the enormous level that we are involved in, including the governments, the generals, the Senate, and the laboratories. So, while we are covering it up (using the conflict in Ukraine) let's make some money meanwhile, for the military complex. So, from 2014 how much money they sent to Ukraine from the taxpayer's money? $400 billion? So, let's continue to cover it up and we turn it against Russia because Russia is a villain.

Let me ask you this, what is the outcome of all of this? And is there any place that I am wrong about?

Scott Ritter: Well, first of all, we will start with this: your facts and your intuition, you're not wrong. You're incomplete and you might have put some priorities on areas that I wouldn't agree with, but fundamentally you are not wrong. You have touched on the essence of the two positions.

Where are we going with this?

The day of negotiation is over. Russia is not going to negotiate. They tried, they tried that for over a decade, as some would say over two decades. In December of last year they gave the United States, NATO, two drafts, treaties, completed documents that said this, what we need is to stop a military operation in Ukraine, we need a guarantee of Ukraine being neutral and we need NATO to basically back off, stop expanding, but more than that Russia said, "it's intolerable to have nations on our periphery like Poland, like the Baltics who receive NATO formations, NATO bases and stuff; we, Russia, have no problem with Poland having the military, Poland is a sovereign nation, Poland can do what it wants to do, Poland can be a member of NATO, we have no problem with the Baltics having militaries or being members of NATO, we wish they weren't, but they can join the European

Community, they can have whatever economic relations they want."

But what Russia is not going to agree with is when a British battalion is on the Lithuanian soil; what bothers Russia is when an American division is on Polish soil because now Russia has to ask "what is the purpose of putting these forces so close to our soil?", especially when NATO has proven to be an offensive organization that has, as part of its mission, a regime change.

We saw NATO use offensive military action to change the regime in Serbia in 1999: they targeted Milosevic for removal, and they removed him. We saw them use offensive military action in Libya in 2011 to remove Gaddafi from power. And so now, when you have the United States committing to a policy of a regime change in Russia, because that is our policy to get rid of Vladimir Putin, and we see NATO expanding, we see NATO signaling out Russia as the number one threat which means that NATO is defined by its ability to respond to this threat, so Russia has every right to say, "we view this expansion of NATO as an existential threat and it has to come to an end."

So what Russia is demanding, and there will be no negotiations on this, Russia is demanding that Ukraine is neutral. They are also demanding, and this is the hint to the future, that Finland remains neutral.

People don't understand the history between Finland and Russia. Let me give you just a brief touch-up. Finland sided with the Nazis in WWII to attack Russia. Now, people say "yes, but that was in response to the short war, 1939–1940, that was fought between Russia and Finland, but that goes back how Finland was created, czar's time etc."

The bottom line, though, is that Finland invaded Russia, the Soviet Union, with the Nazis. They sought to capture Saint Petersburg; they participated in the siege of Leningrad when million Russians died; 440 days of horror. They sought to attack through Soviet Russian soil to threaten Kola Peninsula where you have Russian strategic military capabilities. So, when the war ended and Finland realized what a mistake they made, they quit the alliance with Germany and suddenly said: "Okay, we want to be friendly with the Soviet Union again."

The Soviets were very kind because what they could have done is terminate Finnish state, they could have occupied Finland and absorbed it as a republic. But they didn't. Instead, they said, you are an independent, sovereign state and what we insist though is on your neutrality; never again can Finnish soil be used as a launching pad for the Western forces to threaten Russia, never again.

This is why Finland is allowed to have territory so close to modern day Saint Petersburg. Think about it, how short your drive is from Saint Petersburg. This is why Finland is allowed to have a border that is just a hop, skip and a jump away from Kola Peninsula. Russia doesn't view Finland as a threat, never has. Russia lives peacefully with Finland. Russia had great economic and political relations with Finland. But now NATO has poisoned Finland's mind, and Finland is now saying we can't be secure, even though Russia has never threatened us, we can't be secure, unless we join NATO. And Russia is saying as loud as they can, if you join NATO, we will destroy you.

Ania K: What will be the outcome?

Scott Ritter: Ukraine will be defeated, decisively. It will no longer exist as it currently exists.

I think Putin has had enough. I watched his speech with great interest, he said there will not be a negotiated settlement, we are not negotiating with anybody, we will finish everything we set out to do. And Putin now is making it clear that Zelensky is part of the Nazi problem. Therefore, denazification means Zelensky is gone. Now, how? We don't know. I think Russia was preserving Zelensky in hopes that he would come to his senses and enter into a negotiated settlement with Russia. Russia is no longer looking for a negotiated settlement.

Watch the full interview.

CHAPTER FOUR

"NATO is a Gang"

| July 28, 2023 |

We, the Heads of State and Government of the North Atlantic Alliance, bound by shared values of individual liberty, human rights, democracy, and the rule of law, have gathered in Vilnius as war continues on the European continent, to reaffirm our enduring transatlantic bond, unity, cohesion, and solidarity at a critical time for our security and international peace and stability.

NATO is a defensive Alliance. It is the unique, essential and indispensable transatlantic forum to consult, coordinate and act on all matters related to our individual and collective security. We reaffirm our iron-clad commitment to defend each other and every inch of Allied territory at all times, protect our one billion citizens, and safeguard our freedom and democracy, in accordance with Article 5 of the Washington Treaty.

We will continue to ensure our collective defense from all threats, no matter where they stem from, based on a 360-degree approach, to fulfil NATO's three core tasks of deterrence and defense, crisis prevention and management, and cooperative security. We adhere to international law and to the purposes and principles of the Charter of the United Nations and are committed to upholding the rules-based international order. This Summit marks a milestone in strengthening our Alliance.

NATO Communique, July 11, 2023

Ania K: *I want to start with something important, and that is NATO and its 14 articles. Article 1 says: "The Parties undertake, as set forth in the Charter of the United Nations, to settle any international dispute in which they may be involved by peaceful means in such a manner that international peace and security and justice are not endangered, and to refrain in their international relations from the threat or use of force in any manner inconsistent with the purposes of the United Nations."*

My question is this: clearly this is article 1, what happens if these articles are not respected? They are not respecting their own article 1.

Scott Ritter: Well, what happens when you are from a club and you make club rules and the everybody decides after a while that these rules are inconvenient, we are just going to disregard them. You know NATO of course is in violation of its own rules. I mean, this is what I call the morality clause of NATO, trying to establish NATO as a legitimate organization, you know, an organization of defense, meaning that the only time NATO would use military force would be if they were attacked and then article 54 comes into play. And so they set out and say we will seek to resolve everything peacefully, we're not an aggressor organization. That clearly isn't the case today. NATO is a violent organization; war is its business. It exists only for war. It exists to use the threat of military force and actual military violence in pursuit of its collective policies and more realistically as an extension of American Foreign and National Security Policy.

You know what they do is they throw lip service out there; their idea of a peaceful resolution would be for Russia to capitulate; Russian capitulation would bring about a peaceful resolution to this problem, but Russia is not going to capitulate because the problem was created by NATO and NATO's members.

We cannot separate the policies of France and Germany from NATO when it comes to the Minsk agreements, and we now know that France and Germany went forward to create the conditions of trapping the Russians in a so- called ceasefire that allowed NATO and Ukraine to stall for time because at the same time when France and Germany are stalling for time to build a Ukrainian army, NATO is building a Ukrainian army, the United States and NATO trainers are building a Ukrainian army. How is that peaceful? And what is the purpose of that Ukrainian army? It's not that I have to speculate; the United States Department of Defense put up a slide that said every 55 days we train a Ukrainian Battalion to NATO standards so they can go here, and they draw an arrow to Eastern Ukraine to fight Russians. So, there is nothing peaceful about NATO, it's a charter, especially Article 1, just shows the hypocrisy of NATO today.

Ania K: *So, in this case if Article 1 is clearly not respected, who is looking over it? Who is the judge of it, to say: "All right NATO, you are not respecting Article 1," is it the United Nations?*

Scott Ritter: No. NATO is not beholden to the United Nations. NATO is a collective security arrangement, a treaty that operates outside the framework of the United Nations, so the Secretary General of the UN has no impact on it. NATO's beholden to no one but it's collective membership, so they please themselves.

Ania K: *So, it's like a gang.*

Scott Ritter: Good job! I like that. Can I steal that because I'm going to use that.

Ania K: *Please do. This is just my simple way of thinking about these things, since I am not an expert.*

Watch the full interview.

CHAPTER FIVE

Tanks, But No Tanks

| January 27, 2023 |

Ukraine's new tanks won't be the instant game-changer some expect.

Those hoping that main battle tanks donated by NATO allies to Ukraine will have an immediate impact in its war with Russia may have to adjust their expectations.

After confirming it will receive deliveries of the American M-1 Abrams, German Leopards and British Challengers, Kyiv is now confronted with the logistical and operational realities of incorporating an assortment of vastly different and complex heavy armor into effective fighting units.

But first, the Ukrainians must factor in the timeline for delivery.

Even the most optimistic estimates say it will take months for the tanks to enter the battlefield in numbers to make a big difference, while in the case of Abrams tanks it could be more than a year before Ukraine is able to deploy them.

Deputy Pentagon press secretary Sabrina Singh said Thursday that the United States would provide Ukraine with an advanced version of the Abrams, the M1A2.

The U.S. does not "have these tanks available in excess in our U.S. stocks," she said, adding it will take "months to transfer" them to Ukraine.

Many analysts say it would make things easier for Ukraine to stick with one kind of tank, and that's what makes Germany's decision to allow Leopards into the fight so important.

Modern main battle tanks are complicated pieces of weaponry. Looking formidable and rugged on the outside, much of their effectiveness on the battlefield comes down to sophisticated electronic and computer systems at their core. Those systems find targets and train the tank's main gun on them.

Maintaining the tanks, repairing them, and supplying the parts necessary requires detailed training all the way from the crews in the vehicles to the logistics trail supporting them, hundreds or maybe thousands of miles from the front lines in eastern Ukraine.

Brad Lendon, *CNN,* January 27, 2023

Ania K: *So many of those "clown governments" are sending tanks to Ukraine, I'm trying to be sarcastic but it's not really funny, it's just you don't know how to approach this subject anymore. Anyway, it looks to me like the La Gande Finale is coming. And here, I would like to ask you what do you think? How will this La Grande Finale look like from the Russian standpoint? How will Russia end this?*

Scott Ritter: Russia will end this well. Russia is ending it right now. Russia mobilized 300,000 troops. They've reorganized their Command Staff, they not only have the manpower sufficient to the task, but it's been equipped with some of the most modern equipment Russia has, and they have a plan, and the plan is being executed as we speak.

Russia has an extended front line with Ukraine. You know, since May [2022], Russia has been running a meat grinder operation in the Bakhmut-Soledar area, estimated 14 brigades of Ukrainian troops that each have between 4 and 5 thousand troops. You do the math, we're talking 80,000–90,000 troops have been sacrificed in the Bakhmut area, which is to Russia's advantage. They're very happy with that result and they are continuing to do that. They are making progress.

A lot of people are saying, "well, you have to wait till the Russians breakthrough in Bakhmut." They don't need to. Bakhmut is the magnet that attracts Ukrainian reserves and then the Ukrainian reserves get ground up. What's happening now is Ukraine has exhausted its reserves. You only have to take a look at the frantic pace of mobilization in Ukraine. The pathetic images of these thugs driving around and grabbing men off the streets and out of their homes in a desperate bid to fill the ranks of depleted force.

And now, Russia is launching offenses in Zaporizhia area, in the south, and having success. Ukraine has to deploy reserves to that area to try to stop that and as soon as they do that the Russians open up at Vuhledar, north of Bakhmut and now as they are having success, Ukraine has to divert forces and then they're going to open up closer to Liman up north, and again Ukrainians don't have any reserves left. What's going to happen is Ukraine is going to extend its forces along a frontage it can't defend; there will be nothing in the rear and, at the appropriate time, the Russians will bring the hammer, which is 10 to 15 divisions that they've built up and they will come in, and it is game over, set, match.

You know, it's not just me saying this. General Zaluzhny, Ukrainian Commander of the Armed Forces, said back last month, in an interview with *The Economist*, that if he doesn't get 300 tanks, 500 infantry fighting vehicles, 500 artillery pieces, he's going to lose the conflict. He straight up said it: "We're going to lose."

All these tanks that are being provided, it's only 140 tanks, it's less than 50 percent of what Zaluzhny said he needed, and they are not all going to come at once. They are going to be parceled out here and there, and everywhere. Some of them may never show up, like the American tank that we promised but we don't have, and we have to build it. Others are going to be pulled out of the warehouse, like the Portuguese and the Spanish tanks that don't work, and they are going to give them anyway. The others are going to be brought in a penny packet in time, 12 here, 14 there, thrown in with crews that don't know how to work them.

It takes 22 weeks to train a modern tank crew. There aren't 22 weeks out there to train these groups.

The Ukrainians used to operate in 3-man tank crews because of automatic loaders. Every tank that's coming is a 4-person crew. Now they need manual loading, that's a whole different concept and approach to fighting the war. Yes, you can teach somebody to do it but is it going to be proficient? Is the crew going to work as a team? Then, the most important thing is how you maintain these tanks? We're talking about a wide variety of tanks. The M1 Abrams, like I said, if it ever comes, uses jet fuel; the others use diesel with their different engines, different packs, different maintenance, different maintenance issues.

The Leopard 2 tanks cannot be maintained by a guy who's trained to maintain the T-72, you need a Leopard 2 maintainer. The Leclerc, the French tank, needs a French maintainer, the British Challenger too, the Italians too are talking about throwing in an Italian tank, that needs maintenance.

So, the stuff shows up with no maintenance capability. They all break, people know that. Anybody who's been involved in tanks knows that they break. Normally you have a whole system designed to pull the tank off in the battlefield with a tank retriever and then people who are trained and equipped to come in and fix it, well, come in and do it on the battlefield. If it needs more, it can be pulled a little bit further back. The Ukrainians don't have that. So, when this stuff breaks, it's got to be taken all the way off the battlefield, back to Poland and Germany and that's just a recipe for disaster.

So, these tanks aren't going to have any impact on the battle-field and when they come to the battlefield they are going to be destroyed. Why?

If you think that the Leopard 2 A6 variant, which is the most modern variant people are talking about, some of the variants are the A5, the A4, some are even Leopard 1. But the A6, it came out in 2007; the Russians began re-modernizing their military in 2008 and 2014, so it could fight NATO. Which means that they are looking at NATO's weaponry and saying, how can we defeat that?

And from 2014 until today, Russia has been building systems specifically designed to destroy NATO's tanks, and they have a lot of them.

So, when the Leopard 2 shows up, even though it might be a qualitative advancement for the Ukrainians, it's not something that makes the Russians afraid. The Russians are not happy about this decision because this will complicate the war, extend the time of the war, cost them lives, but they are confident in their victory. They are going to destroy these tanks. That's just the statement of fact.

That's what Zelenski said. He is only getting less than 50 percent of the tanks he requested; he wants 300, he gets about 140-150, he wanted 500 infantry vehicles he will get 240, he wanted 500 artillery pieces, he will get about 130. So, he is not getting what he wants.

Now, we go to President Zelenski who brought this down to the basic essence. He said, "if I don't get the M1 Abrams by August, then it's too late." Too late for what? He knows what's going on. The war is over. He lost. What he doesn't realize is that these tanks are purely a political gesture on the part of the Collective West to save face, to say "we tried to do everything we could to help these people."

But there is nothing they can do to help.

There are not enough tanks. There is not enough time. There is not enough support.

Now they are talking about aircraft. If you want to see something that's more pathetic than NATO's effort to provide tanks to Ukraine, watch NATO try to provide aircrafts.

The fact of the matter is, the Russians are in the process of shaping the battlefield to their singular advantage. They have sufficient resources available to exploit any opportunities that emerge as they continue to press the Ukrainians and, as Zelenski said, this war is going to be over by August. That's what is going on.

Watch the full interview.

CHAPTER SIX

Men Die Hard

| October 28, 2022 |

It's evening in Kyiv. Here's what you need to know.

Progress hasn't come easily in recent days for Ukrainian troops in the eastern part of the country, while the nation's capital deals with another day of power outages brought on by Russian strikes.

If you're just joining us, here's what you need to know about the war in Ukraine today:

Kyiv's power held hostage: Emergency power outages continue in Kyiv as the city struggles to repair "significant damage" from attacks on energy infrastructure. The deputy head of Russia's Security Council threatened that energy stability was only possible through recognizing Moscow's demands, including its recent annexations, which are condemned by the United Nations and other international bodies.

Ukrainian counteroffensive slows in the east: The advance of Ukrainian troops in the eastern Luhansk region is "not going as fast as we would like," according to a regional official, due to weather and thousands of mobilized Russian reservists. Luhansk is one of four Ukrainian regions Russian President Vladimir Putin claimed to have annexed last month.

The battle for Kherson: The southern Kherson region is a focal point in the war, after weeks of gains raised the

> *possibility that Ukraine could retake the regional capital from Russian forces. Moscow sent as many as 1,000 mobilized personnel to help hold the west bank of the Dnipro River, Ukraine's military said, and Russia reported a more stable situation, with less artillery fire and no Ukrainian counterattacks.*
>
> Rob Picheta, Tara Subramaniam, Adrienne Vogt, and Matt Meyer, *CNN*, October 28, 2022

Ania K: *How much longer they will be dragging this conflict? Can you give us a time frame?*

Scott Ritter: Well, let's start off by saying that Russia isn't operating on any calendar that I'm aware of. I have yet to see a Russian official say, we need to achieve x by this date, because they are outcome driven. So, any answer I give you is based upon my assessment on how long it will take Russia to achieve an outcome, the stated outcome being demilitarization, denazification and basically creating a neutral Ukraine; then, based upon an assessment of what I think Russia will be doing.

But Russia doesn't respond to me. I don't pick up the phone and tell Putin: "Hurry it up on the carousel in front, boss, Ritter needs you to go faster because he is committed to a date." They don't care. They've shown they don't care.

I think they wanted this to be done quickly, that's the nature of the special military operation that was based upon the premise that there wouldn't be resistance, not to the level that was achieved or provided by the Ukrainians Then they shifted to an altered campaign that focused solely on Donbas, but they weren't willing to take the casualties necessary to liberate Donbas quickly.

So it became more of a protracted struggle as they literally ground their way through Ukrainian defenses, killing a whole bunch of Ukrainians, minimizing Russian losses, but that provided NATO time to spend billions of dollars' worth of equipment in allowing

Ukraine to reconstitute an army that took advantage of the fact that the Russians had transitioned from the quick easy victory to a grinding operation. NATO didn't increase the number of resources that were inadequate to the scope of the tasks they were trying to accomplish, and the Ukrainians with this new NATO army launched their counterattack; they retook Kherson, they seized part of the Kherson, but the Russians have consolidated their defenses, and the Ukrainians are literally committing suicide on the Russian defenses. It's like watching zombies running into spikes, it's tragic.

Now, Russia is building up and it's up to Russia to decide when. I mean, this is a decision that commanders make on the ground. They have a new General, Surovikin, General Armageddon. He is the guy who makes the decisions, and he's made it clear, in his various presentations, that he is a mission-oriented guy, but he is driven by conditions that will minimize the casualties among the civilians and minimize Russian losses. He is not willing to throw away Russian lives.

War is a dirty, nasty business. And believe it or not, even though human life is fragile, men die hard, men don't die easy.

So, anybody who is out there looking for a quick Russian victory, hey guys, Ukrainian men aren't just going to stand up and take a bullet in the head for your convenience, they're going to die hard, they're going to fight. Humans hold onto life; they scratch, and troops that are in a desperate situation will often times be empowered with the virility of desperation and they fight hard. They die hard. It's not easy to kill a person. It's really not that easy.

So, this war is going to take time. I can't sit here and say, this should happen or that should happen. I can't say the Russians want this to happen by that day, etc. What I can do is to say that the military situation on the ground is related to the geopolitical economic reality that encompasses this conflict. The Ukrainians are not able to sustain this fight without the continuous, non-stop

provision of money and material from the West, and we're seeing that the West is losing the appetite to continue feeding this
baby with black caviar. You know, they were happy to give it
but now the caviar costs too much, they're running out of caviar,
babies are demanding more. They don't have it.

And then, the other problem is, Ukraine itself is dying. There
is no glee in this. Ukraine is dying. The nation is dying. The
electricity is off, it's not coming back on. The infrastructure is
destroyed, even when the electricity wants to come back on,
the nation is destroyed. Done. Finished. And this is the reality
that the Ukrainian Army is operating in. The Ukrainian Army is
totally depended upon outside assistance. The nation of Ukraine
is no longer able to sustain that military force.

So as the nation dies, as the West turns away, the Ukrainian
Army will wither.

This winter is going to be extraordinarily difficult for these
Ukrainian soldiers.

First of all, they've burned up all of their offensive strike capability. The notion that Ukraine is going to carry out some sort of
winter offensive, once the ground solidifies, is absurd. The reality is, snow is coming or, as they say in *The Game of Thrones,*
"winter is coming," and when these Ukrainians move, because
right now they're dug in, if you take a look at the videos, there is
greenery, there's trees, there's leaves in these forest belts that are
their lines of defense, and the Russians have to send the drones
up, and they're looking for them, and when they find them, they
get them, but they are not getting anybody. In wintertime, there's
going to be no leaves, they're going to come out of their bunker
and [... go off and do what they do, making footprints when
they go out, and when they come back]. They're going to get
in vehicles. Vehicles are going to arrive with a giant track set
that points exactly to where they are, and the Russians are going
to be up there with their drones going "gotcha!," and they are

going to take them out with artillery, pound them to death, kill everybody. Men may die hard, artillery kills harder.

And they are going to just blow these guys to hell. And then, the Russians are going to come in because now they have the resources to carry out doctrinal advance, doctrinal offensive operations.

And so, what I think you are going to see is a culmination of the collapse of western will and ability to sustain Ukraine, the collapse of Ukraine's ability to sustain the army, and the Russians grinding down the army, and that's going to sequence into sort of a rapid Russian military/political victory.

I think the Russians will have the Ukrainians on the run. The only problem is, I think they'll have them on the run this winter but then, the Russians will run into the same problems, they're going to extend their lines. Let's say the Russians do what I think they're going to do, which is to save Transnistria problem and complete the job of destroying Ukraine as a modern, industrial state by taking Odessa, linking up to Transnistria, cutting Ukraine off from ports, strangling Ukraine economically. I think after stabilizing the front, that's their next objective. It's more important than Kharkov.

So, I think, they are going to do that, but in doing that they're extending the line of contact with Ukraine by 1200 km. They need troops now to hold that line and to hold Odessa. So, they have sufficient forces available to do that, but they're going to need more troops for the next stage. Now, the next stage is not going to be as difficult because the Ukrainian Army would have been destroyed, but there still will be people fighting.

And here is another thing; there will be a great potential of Poland to think, "Oh now, it's the time to make a move on Western Ukraine," especially if the Ukrainians have overextended themselves, haven't brought up sufficient forces to carry on, and Poland may make the move.

This is why Russia has positioned 80,000 troops in Belarus. This is why the Belarusian Army is moving up and forming a join operational group to prepare, to respond to that, and that may be the trigger that can make the Russians come and take Odessa. And then, the Belarus operational group may come down and secure Western Ukraine and strangle Kiev.

Who knows what's going to happen. I've just described one scenario, General Armageddon may be chuckling going, "You're a clever boy, Ritter, but that ain't the plan, I have a better plan." I don't know what it is. It's his plan, not mine. But I do believe that all the circumstances we've talked about will reach a culmination in the spring, the early summer from a military standpoint. And then, from a political standpoint, I do think the Russians have this thing tied up with a nice little bow on the box by default. I don't see Ukraine surviving past the fall of 2023. They may collapse sooner, but I just can't envision how 1) Russia would allow this struggle to continue that much longer, because that is a strain on Russia and 2) the European political landscape is going to be radically transformed over the course of this winter. Governments may no longer be in government and Europe's ability or willingness or desire to provide the same level of support may no longer be an option.

Watch the full interview.

CHAPTER SEVEN

Waiting for the (Nuclear) Suntan

| October 12, 2022 |

Why NATO Needs to Plan for Nuclear War

As the alliance meets this week, leaders must discuss how they will react if Russia uses weapons of mass destruction.

NATO defense ministers will gather this week for a ministerial meeting, but one topic of discussion will be anything but routine: the risk that Russian President Vladimir Putin might use nuclear weapons in Europe. The recent massive, disproportionate missile attacks launched against Ukraine in response to the truck bombing of the Kerch Bridge reinforce the notion that the Kremlin remains unpredictable.

Although Russian use of weapons of mass destruction (WMD) against non-nuclear Ukraine seems unlikely for several reasons, including the fact that it may frustrate Russia's broader goals, Western military officials can and must think through their potential responses. Doing so is inherently difficult given the many variables in play, but there are options that would punish Moscow and safeguard alliance interests without necessarily propelling the West up a nuclear escalation ladder.

John R. Deni, *Foreign Policy,* October 12, 2020

Ania K: *Will Russia direct their weapons on the decision-making centers in the United States?*

Scott Ritter: First of all, Russia is talking about conventional weapons. When Russia says, "We are going to hit the decision-making centers," they're talking about using Kinzhal hypersonic weapons, non-nuclear weapons. There is a lot Russia can do before they go nuclear, they're not a pathetic power, they're actually a very capable power who has developed extremely modern, effective, non-nuclear weapons systems that can be employed.

But here is the thing—once a single nuclear weapon is used, Russia will blow everything up, because there's no such a thing as a limited nuclear war in Russia's mindset. The West, we mirror image down to Russia, we keep talking about how the Russians have a doctrine of escalate to de-escalate, that the Russians will seek to use a nuclear weapon to escalate the conflict, intimidating us to de-escalate, so we need to be prepared to escalate first, use nuclear weapons first and get the Russians to back down.

I would just say, read Russian doctrine: If we use nuclear weapons we might as well get drunk, sit out in the backyard and wait for the big 200,000 degree suntan because it's going to go boom, the flash is going to hit us and we're going to die. Russia doesn't play games; nuclear deterrence means that you have to convince your opponent that the consequences of using nuclear weapons are so dire that you would never consider using nuclear weapons. But in order for that to work, you have to be serious about doing it. Russia is serious that if nuclear weapons are used against it, it will terminate all life on earth, all life, all life is going to end. Putin has said it, we will go to heaven as martyrs, you will go wherever people who started it will go. Russia is not going to start a nuclear war, but Russia is going to end it, not to win but to destroy the world. That is what nuclear deterrence is about.

If you believe that Russia is not serious about this, that Russia would back down, then Russia is not deterring anything. The West needs to wake up to the fact that there can be no talk about using nuclear weapons.

I don't have a lot of respect for people in Pentagon but I would say this, when Mark Millie, who is the Chairman of Joint Chiefs of Staff, was questioned about the Trump period, at the end of the Trump era, when President Trump was deemed by some to have gone off the rails and lost ability for rational thinking, and some people thought in order to preserve his presidency he might do something crazy like order a nuclear strike, the answer that Millie gave to that question was heartwarming. He said, you know, there is a lot that has to go on for a nuclear strike to take place and it has to be a lawful order, and just because the President says to launch, it doesn't mean it's a lawful order. We have to look at the case, what is the military necessity of this? Does the launch meet our doctrinal requirements? I mean, has something occurred for this use, to need to use nuclear weapon, and if it's just a President waking up saying, I want to launch a nuke that doesn't meet our doctrine, then we don't do it.

We also have to talk about proportionality, meaning, are there other means to respond to whatever threat has occurred? Is that use of a nuclear weapon disproportional to the threat that has manifested itself?

There is just a whole bunch of questions that have to be asked and answered throughout the chain of command. It's the duty and the responsibility from everybody in the nuclear chain of command to ask these questions and, if they are not answered to your satisfaction, not to execute the order because it is unlawful order with horrific consequences.

Look, American military officers are professional, and while all of them want to go home to their wives and their children, those who have assumed the mantle of nuclear guardians, so to speak, will, if called upon, execute their responsibility, which means they will launch the nuclear weapons if the conditions have been met. But if the conditions haven't been met, they're not just simply going to do something because a madman tells them to do it.

So that gives me hope that we won't see some stupidity. That's why I am convinced there won't be a preemptive NATO strike, because it's not in the doctrine. The B-61 bombs belong to us. Those weapons are never leaving their storage. Right now, there may be one weapon coming out, where teams go through an operational check to make sure that they want to make the weapon ready for war and demonstrate that they know how to do that, but there's not going to be a release of the weapon, every weapon put on the aircraft will be a dummy weapon. There is no way that an American officer would do this.

Now, here's the problem. I don't trust the Poles. The Poles are insane. They are crazy. No disrespect but they are insane. They're like Ukrainians, absolutely bonkers, that's why they can never be entrusted with nuclear weapons because if you give the Poles the nuclear bomb and you give them the ability to launch it when they want to launch it, they would launch it because they are insane. I don't trust them. I don't trust a lot of nations anymore. But right now, I trust the United States when it comes to nuclear weapons because even President Biden has said it repeatedly, we don't want that, that's not what we want, we're not heading this direction.

So that's the optimism that I have.

Watch the full interview.

CHAPTER EIGHT

Arms Control Is My Business

| July 1, 2022 |

U.S.-Russian Dialogue Remains Paused as Putin Wields Nuclear Threats

In the opening days of Russia's war on Ukraine, President Vladimir Putin ordered Russia's nuclear forces to move to a heightened alert status and threatened any country thinking of interfering on Kyiv's behalf with nuclear retaliation.

"No matter who tries to stand in our way, or all the more so create threats for our country and our people, they must know that Russia will respond immediately, and the consequences will be such as you have never seen in your entire history," Putin said Feb. 24, the first day of the invasion of Ukraine. He again issued this threat April 27, saying that any interference will be met with "lightning-fast" retaliatory strikes.

Neither the United States nor the North Atlantic Treaty Organization (NATO) have made reciprocal moves to change the alert status of their nuclear forces.

Within two days of the start of the invasion, the United States paused the bilateral strategic stability dialogue with Russia in which the two sides have in the past discussed nuclear arms control.

However, in June, both Putin and U.S. President Joe Biden communicated a desire to hold this dialogue once more, though U.S. and Russian officials have simultaneously expressed skepticism that this will occur anytime soon.

"Even as we rally the world to hold Russia accountable for its brutal and unprovoked war on Ukraine, we must continue to engage Russia on issues of strategic stability," Biden wrote in a June 2 letter to the Arms Control Association. "Our progress must continue beyond the [2010 New Strategic Arms Reduction Treaty] New START extension," he added.

Later in June, Putin expressed that "Russia is open to dialogue on ensuring strategic stability, preserving agreements on the non-proliferation of weapons of mass destruction, and improving the situation in arms control."

Shannon Bugos, *Arms Control Association,* July 19, 2022

Ania K: *Scott, if you would have a chance to have a phone conversation with President Putin, and in that conversation, you can share whatever you like and, let's say he would ask you for your advice on this current situation. What would you tell him?*

Scott Ritter: I would say that I am in no position to advise him on this special military operation that's ongoing in Ukraine, that this is Russia's business, only Russia can decide what to do in that extent.

What I would say is this: Mr. President, I am somebody with some experience in arms control and I did participate in a very successful exercise of arms control between the United States and the Soviet Union back in the late 1980s and early 1990s, the intermediate nuclear forces treaty, that helped walk us away from the brunt of nuclear annihilation.

I would say, Mr. President, I know you are focused on winning this fight in Ukraine, I know you're concerned about NATO expansion, but I would advise you to begin working with whatever outlet you can in the United States to initiate a meaningful conversation about real arms control because the situation in Europe is only going to get more dangerous. You have proven that you are able to operate in a manner which does not put you in a position where you need to consider using nuclear weapons, so it's not as though you're in a panic mode and saying, Ritter, I'm sorry we have to use nuclear weapons.

At some point in time, Russia and the United States are going to have meaningful arms control or else the world is going to end. Right now, it's very difficult because the United States, as a government, isn't reaching out, but you know there are ways that Russia can interact with the West. For example, I would advise the President to have his Duma hold hearings on arms control and invite western experts non-governmental people, but western experts, to come in and testify about arms control. What the concerns of the West are to start educating themselves as to what the western mindset is, what's going on in America, what issues would have to be overcome for the United States to consider once again embarking down this path [of disarmament], so the Russian Parliament could then advice the Russian Foreign Ministry or the Russian Military about coming up with ideas on how Russia could be proactive on how Russia could make arms control attractive to the West.

These are things that I would talk about. It's none of my business what's going on in Ukraine, I'm in no position to advice Russia about anything. Arms control is my business, it is my passion, and I would advise the Russian President to begin the process of informing Russia about the need for arms control.

Watch the full interview.

CHAPTER NINE

Ukrainian Nationalism Is Just a Euphemism for Nazism

| September 8, 2023 |

Ukraine's Bandera Itch

The Russian invasion of Ukraine on February 24, 2022 has been justified by Russian President Vladimir Putin as a "special military operation" with a few barbed purposes, among them cleaning the country's stables of Nazis. As with so many instances of history, it was not entirely untrue, though particularly convenient for Moscow. At the core of many a nationalist movement beats a reactionary heart, and the trauma-strewn stretch that is Ukrainian history is no exception.

A central figure in this drama remains Stepan Bandera, whose influence during the Second World War have etched him into the annals of Ukrainian history. His appearance in the Russian rationale for invading Ukraine has given his spirit a historical exit clause, something akin to rehabilitation. This has been helped by the scant coverage, and knowledge of the man outside the feverish nationalist imaginings that continue to sustain him…

Bandera offers a slice of historical loathing and reverence for a good number of parties: as a figure of the Holocaust, an opportunistic collaborator, a freedom fighter. Even within Ukraine, the split between the reverential West and the loathing East remained. In January 2010, Ukrainian

> *President Viktor Yushchenko declared Bandera a Hero of Ukraine.*
>
> *In 2020, Poland and Israel jointly rebuked the city government of Kyiv via its ambassadors for sporting banners connected with the nationalist figure. Bandera's portrait made an appearance on a municipal building at the conclusion of a January 1 march honouring the man's 111th birthday, with hundreds of individuals in attendance.*
>
> Binoy Kampmark, *CounterPunch*, September 14, 2023

Ania K: *So, here I have a question that might be strange, but I don't really think that Nazis had lost WWII, they were relocated to Argentina and some other places and they took on a different identity and went on to create families; then from those families they put certain people into positions, very important strategic positions that are now running many countries.*

Do you think that Nazis will ever be removed from this planet?

Scott Ritter: I mean the thing about Nazis is there is a physical aspect to it, as you've described it, and then there is an ideological aspect of it.

One of the big problems at the end of World War II was that we, being the West, almost immediately went into an anti-Soviet struggle and, in doing so, we made it possible that the people that we were formally fighting against were now being seen as potential allies because our new enemy, the Soviet Union, was the enemy of these people. So this allowed us to go through various mental gymnastics where we could take General Gehlen for instance, who ran Nazi intelligence on the east front, and allowed him to become a part of a new German intelligence organization subordinated to the United States that ran Ukrainian nationalists who stayed behind in western Ukraine, in Belarus, in eastern Poland, and the organization of Ukrainian nationalists, the IPA, they were there, tens of thousands remained behind being controlled by Nazis, working for the Nazis for the benefit of the Nazis, who then got released by the Germans and taken over by the CIA, and so now they are working for the CIA to do their nefarious tasks.

So already we have Nazis on the ground, working for the CIA, we have Nazis fleeing, about 120,000 Ukrainian nationalists fled to Nazi Germany as they retreated out of Ukraine, they went back to Germany and many of them, most of them, none of them were turned over to the Soviets after the war.

The 14th SS division, the Galician Division, surrendered en masse to the Germans or to the British and the British pretty much pardoned them all and sent them to England and Canada, sent Nazis, honest-to-God Nazi SS members to Canada, to England; others dispersed there, that was a whole wave that came to the United States.

As I keep talking about it, 60 miles down the road Ellenville, NY, there's an organization for Ukrainian nationalists summer camp where they indoctrinate children every year, they just run a camp through there, they have hero monuments, "Slava Ukraina" and the "glory to the heroes" symbols of Ukraine flanked by four statues, Stepan Bandera and Roman Shukhyevich on the side, the greatest mass murderers in modern history, right there, glorified as heroes for these Ukrainian Nazis who live in America and perpetuate their ideology. They just took a photograph of the summer camp this summer, dated June, where they had the kids wearing their brown Nazi uniforms, holding up portraits of Stepan Bandera and banners with Nazi symbology on it. It's insane what's going on right now.

So, they reside here, they reside in Canada, the Great Britain, Australia and Germany, they are everywhere. So even if Russia was to eradicate all the Right Sector, Svoboda Party, Azov Battalion members and kill them all in Ukraine, the cancer still exists overseas, paid for and supported by the CIA. And as these people grow up, not only in Ukraine, I think I've talked about this before, that about 200,000 Banderites were captured by the Soviets at the end when they finally crushed the resistance and they were imprisoned in the Gulag, but in 1959 Nikita Khrushchev did his destalinization, you know he had his speech and basically started condemning Stalin and trying to turn a fresh page, and so he opened up the doors of the Gulag and released those political prisoners. Now, some of them were political prisoners but many of them were mass murderers, the people that participated, facilitated, collaborated with Ukrainians who slaughtered Jews.

When I say slaughtered, I mean—people really have to do their research; there are photographs you have to look at, as the Ukrainian is pointing the rifle at the mother holding her child, threatening to knock their brains out and put her to death. That's what they do. That's what they did. These are heartless scum.

Then, they were put into the Gulag, then they were released from the Gulag and then they were allowed back into the society where they worked their way up through the Ukrainian ranks, intimidating people—that's what the Ukrainian nationalist do, they knock at the door, if you don't support us, we'll kill you, your wife, your children. That happened throughout Soviet times…this is all being done, funded by the CIA, using the diaspora. The diaspora retains contact with these Ukrainians, it's done in the guise of cultural exchanges or whatever they want to call it, with the CIA's funding money.

It was the CIA that funneled money to these people up to 1990, after that money was taken over by other sources of income that were not directly tied to the CIA but still were seeking the cause of promoting this ideology as a way of undermining the Soviet Union.

I tell you this; they lost but they didn't die. And they are being reborn.

There is no doubt that we defeated the Nazi ideology in 1945, but we didn't kill them all and we didn't run them to the ground, and we didn't eliminate them, we didn't liquidate them, we allowed them to survive. We've fostered them to the West.

The internal Canadian discussion that took place in the 1940s are far different from the discussions that take place today, because in the 1940s they were going, "We don't want these Nazis." They called them what they were. They said, "You are Nazis, this is SS, we don't want them here." But the Commonwealth, the British, put pressure on, and they received them. They were received by the large Ukrainian diaspora that already existed and they took over that diaspora, imprinting upon them their mentality, ideology and today we have people like Chrystia Freeland, Senior Canadian Government Official. She's a Nazi, 100 percent Nazi. She lies about her grandfather's past as a Nazi propagandist. She was raised in the scouting system which is a pro-Bandera scouting system. She's been indoctrinated in totality and her policies, and the policies of the Canadian government reflect that.

The cancer exists in America, it exists in Canada, it exists everywhere.

Anybody that allows the Ukrainian diaspora is clearly linked to the ideology of Stepan Bandera and the organization of Ukrainian nationals to exist and produce people who are then brought up through the system to attain positions of high governmental authority.

In the United States we have Victoria Nuland, she is a Nazi.

Pretty much anybody who is Ukrainian is a Nazi.

Ukrainian nationalism is just a euphemism for Nazism.

Watch the full interview.

CHAPTER TEN

Hammer Time

| March 13, 2023 |

Ukraine eyes an offensive around Bakhmut, as Russian momentum stalls.

Russian forces are depleted in Bakhmut and a Ukrainian counter-offensive could soon be launched, one of Kyiv's top generals has said, raising the prospect of an unlikely turnaround in the besieged city.

Oleksandr Syrskyi, the commander of Ukraine's land forces, said on his Telegram channel Thursday that "[Russians] are losing significant forces [in Bakhmut] and are running out of energy."

"Very soon, we will take advantage of this opportunity, as we did in the past near Kyiv, Kharkiv, Balakliya and Kupyansk," he said.

His comments come days after Ukraine's President Volodymyr Zelensky made a surprise trip to the front lines of the Donetsk region, and will raise hopes in the West that Kyiv's contentious decision to keep troops in Bakhmut will pay dividends.

A counter-offensive has seemed an unlikely prospect for several weeks, as forces from Russia's Wagner mercenary group bombarded Bakhmut and edged closer toward seizing control of the city.

> *But that effort has come at a considerable cost to man-power and resources, and now appears to have slowed.*
>
> Rob Picheta, Vasco Cotovio, Olga Voitovych, and
> Svitlana Vlasova, *CNN,* March 24, 2023

Ania K: *What does it really mean for Ukraine if they succeed in this counter offensive?*

Scott Ritter: The important thing about this battle is to understand that Ukraine has committed their strategic resources to this fight, so this is literally an existential fight for Ukraine, for Donbas.

Russia has committed Wagner and some supporting units, but in terms if Russia were to lose…well, first of all, what does "losing" mean? That they fail to take Bahamut? How would we define Russian defeat? Because what Ukrainians are doing, they are trying to fight for their survival right now, trying to stop the Russian advance. So, the victory for Ukraine would be that they have bloodied the Russian nose and stopped the Russians in Bakhmut. But what about elsewhere? There is still a continuous line of contact from Kherson up to Kharkov and beyond, and the Russians are advancing there as well.

So, I think a Ukrainian victory forestalls a Russian victory. I don't think the Ukrainians are in a position to reverse.

Now, we could be wrong if they are able to somehow achieve the collapse of Wagner and then carry out a counterattack that recaptured Bakhmut, Soledar, and all that. This could have a deep psychological impact on the Russians.

But that's not going to happen.

First of all, everybody is talking about a Ukrainian counteroffensive. Understand that to move a brigade you need roads. There is only one road leading into Bakhmut right now and it's under continuous fire by the Russians, and the Russians may capture that road. People are talking about 19 brigades, that's something I've read about—16 infantry or mechanized infantry, 3 artillery brigades. You can't jam 19 brigades into a small space, the roads can't handle it, there's not enough room, and you just become a big target.

So, I think that 19 brigades…it's a highly inflated number, it may include some supporting attacks on the flanks, etc., but it's not that easy to go on the offensive, you need a lot of gas, you need a train that supports it, you need roads that will support the logistical sustainability of this conflict and…the Russians aren't stupid.

Every Russian officer who is on the front lines right now, when they look to the left or to the right, they have Russians next to them, they have units that are within interlocking fields of fire; behind them, they have another line of defense and artillery ready to rain down.

So, any Ukrainian attack isn't going to be what happened in September, when the lines were thinly held and there was nothing behind, so if you penetrated the line, you can drive 20 kilometers without any stopping. And here, the Ukrainians— even before they get to the line—are going to be hammered by Russian artillery and air power.

Hammered.

So, whenever a unit crosses, it will be broken up beforehand.

Let's say they find a Russian entrenchment and they lock it in, and they penetrate through the first line of defense, now they're going to hit the second line of defense, and that second line of defense is going to have fire support dedicated to it; so now they're going to get pounded again. Meanwhile a counterattack is going to occur, because the Russians are defending doctrinally, they'll have a counterattack force that will pinch off the flank, cut off these forces and kill them all.

Now, the Ukrainians might have another brigade behind that will attack through there, and then we get into this fight where each attack advances further, and they can put more troops in, but eventually the attacks are going to break down, and it becomes too expensive for the Ukrainians.

I just don't envision the Ukrainians having the military capability to break through the three lines of Russian defenses. You're going to need overwhelming artillery. I don't see that happening.

Even if the Ukrainian army brings all their artillery ammunition to give that kind of fire, the Russians aren't yielding the battle space, which means every time the Ukrainians fire, Russian counter battery fire is going to be coming in, Russian air power is going to be coming in, and you're going to get into this battle where the Ukrainian artillery is going to be attritted at very high levels. So, as the battle goes on, the Ukrainians are going to be bleeding out everything, and then the question is their sustainability. If you're going to enter this kind of fight, this war of attrition, you better have far more resources than your opponent. And the Ukrainians don't. No matter what they have, they will never have anything that matches what the Russians can prepare and remember that we're talking about a situation where the Russians are on the defense, so they accrue an automative three to one advantage, just from that standpoint.

So, the people who are talking about a Ukrainian offensive are insane. That is the worst thing Ukrainians can do.

Watch the full interview.

CHAPTER ELEVEN

Military Math

| April 22, 2022 |

Russia-Ukraine war: List of key events on day 58

As the Russia-Ukraine war enters its 58th day, we take a look at the main developments.

Russia plans to take full control of Donbas and Southern Ukraine as part of the second phase of the military operation, the deputy commander of Russia's central military district said, the Interfax news agency reported.

Ukrainian fighters cling to their last redoubt in Mariupol after Russian President Vladimir Putin declared the port city "liberated."

Ukraine President Volodymyr Zelenskyy said Russian forces control most of Mariupol but Ukrainian troops remain in a part of it. About 120,000 civilians were blocked from leaving, he said.

Putin alone can decide the fate of civilians still trapped in Mariupol, Mayor Vadym Boychenko said, adding that satellite images of a mass grave site were proof Russians were burying bodies to hide the toll.

Russian forces captured 42 villages in the eastern Donetsk region, an aide to Zelenskyy's chief of staff said.

Russian forces are reportedly advancing towards Kramatorsk, also in the east, which continues to be hit by rocket attacks.

> *The mayor of Kharkiv said the city is under intense bombardment.*
>
> *Ukrainian Deputy PM Iryna Vereshchuk says no humanitarian corridors will be open across Ukraine on Friday "due to the danger on the routes today."*
>
> *Al Jazeera,* April 22, 2022

Ania K: *Is Russia going to win this conflict? How will this end?*

Scott Ritter: We're entering the third month of a war that nobody believed would last more than a month. No one did. Many thought, myself included, that is going to be won a lot quicker. I was surprised about three things actually.

One was the soft approach taken by the Russians going in. I understand why they did it. I think history will show us it was a fundamental mistake because it was made on flawed assumptions. You know that Russians arrested 150 officers from the FSB that belong to the Fifth Department that's responsible for doing the intelligence preparations of the battlefield in Ukraine. This group apparently told the Russian leadership that we control certain Ukrainian generals who are going to keep their troops in the barracks and we have bought mayors who are going to ensure that we have the support of the public. This is why the Russians did what they call the "bucket of water"; they flow down the hill, take the path of the least resistance. So they put those poor boys on convoy and said, "Drive until somebody stops you, just keep on driving," and they did.

The Ukrainians didn't stay in their barracks, and the mayors weren't going to support them, and these initial convoys got extended and ambushed and slaughtered. It was horrible. That was a huge mistake by the Russians. So that's one.

Two. I don't think anybody expected, and we should have, this is a fundamental failure of analysis on my part and on everybody's part, that the Ukrainian military turned out to be a lot more professional and a lot more capable and a lot more willing to sacrifice than people thought. I think some people thought, myself included, that once you take out a few elite units that the Ukrainian military will fall like a house of cards and that they would surrender because the Russians are going to come in with their doctrine.

The other thing ... is that the Russian doctrine—and again, history teaches, it's amazing how once reality hits you, you suddenly remember the lessons of history—the Russians were fighting WWII, because there was never a major land combat in the Cold War, it was really an adaptation of WWII tactics through the Cold War and then it continued, the Russian doctrine, the exercises they ran in the fall (moving major tanks, etc.).

I think the Russians were educated that doctrine has to be modified because a capable enemy with good weapons and good training and good leadership will slaughter you if you come at them like that.

So, the Russians haven't changed their way, that's why there was such a big pause between the withdrawal from Kiev and moving in, because the Russians had to retrain their guys.

Putin said it best: "We are fighting a very literal war," and what he meant was "by the book."

And now we come back down to the basics of military math. When you have two sides that are relatively equal, what happens is you get into a grinding match, then one side starts to crumble and the other side gets invested, they can reinforce.

It's the same thing with Napoleonic warfare, if you remember the armies marched toward others in straight lines, then they fired, until one side ground the other side down, then they outflanked, they rolled it up and it was done. That's what's happening right now.

The advantage is all Russia. Ukraine has nothing left. Well, they say, the West is sending them stuff. The U.S. is sending 72 artillery pieces to replace over 1400 that have been destroyed. The math just isn't there.

Even if the Ukrainians brought all 72 to the field, which they will not because a lot of them are going to be destroyed on the way, but let's say 72 miraculously made it, how long are they going to survive? Because they are up against hundreds.

So, they get in the fight and let's say these are the best trained groups and the best guns and every time they fire 72 rounds, they kill 72 Russian artillery pieces and every time the Russians fire, because they are incompetent, they only kill 12, so 72 to 12, now it isn't 72 anymore, it's 60.

60 fires minus 12. It [isn't] 60 anymore, it's 48. And eventually it is zero and it's still hundreds [with Russia].

That's the reality.

The Russians have said, we are not doing the frontal assault and losing a lot of guys anymore; what we're doing is taking advantage of all the advantage we enjoy because it is also about maneuver, it's not just attacking the enemy, the maneuver is also your ability to go back and rest.

Guess who gets to go back and rest? The Russians.

Guess who doesn't? The Ukrainians. There's nowhere for them to rest.

Guess who gets to go back and fall in on hot showers, hot food and fuel? The Russians. The Ukrainians have got none of that. And this is all a cumulative effect.

The Russians right now are just fighting this very slow, deliberate battle.

You listen to the Russians when they said that they've captured hundreds of villages. These are not villages, these are reinforced fortresses, all these villages have had trenches dug in, concrete poured in, these are fortified positions, and the Russians are taking one at the time.

And then the Russians casualties, they're losing one dead, four wounded today, four wounded the next day. The Ukrainians they're losing 60 dead, 100 wounded every day. And again, eventually military math comes into play, and you're just going to go through it until there's nobody left.

So that's where we are right now. We are in the middle of the Russians using every advantage they have in a slow, deliberate battle where the outcome is guaranteed.

The Russians aren't going to make any more mistakes. The days of the Russians allowing one of their convoys to go off and get ambushed are over. That will never happen again. Because too many people died.

When you hear Peskov say: "The losses are terrible...," that doesn't mean they suffered 20,000 killed. That means they suffered 3,000–5,000 dead, that is terrible.

There are now 3,000–5,000 mothers in Russia who lost their kids.

Trust me, it's even worse for the Ukrainians.

Watch the full interview.

CHAPTER TWELVE

Running on Empty

| October 31, 2023 |

> ### *U.S. News & World Report: The Russian Army Is Right Now the Strongest in the World*
>
> *In a recent survey conducted by "U.S. News & World Report," the Russian army has earned the distinction of being declared the most formidable military force globally. This recognition stems from an in-depth evaluation of countries' military capabilities, as determined by participants in a global survey, particularly in the "Strength" sub-category.*
>
> *The United States secured the second position in this comprehensive global ranking of military power, with China following closely in third place. Israel's military prowess earned it the fourth position, while South Korea emerged as the fifth-ranked nation.*
>
> *Ukraine, a country that has been in the global spotlight due to geopolitical tensions, secured the sixth place. Notably, other prominent nations like Iran, Great Britain, Germany, and Turkey also found themselves among the top ten military powers globally.*
>
> Sededin Dedovic, *Financial World,* October 31, 2023

Ania K: *The European arms industry is not able to meet Ukrainian needs for artillery ammunition. To provide Ukraine with enough artillery ammunition the European military industrial complex will need between 7 to 14 years. This opinion was* *presented by the Ukrainian portal "Defense Express," which specializes in the subjects of weapons. The journalists analyzed reports by NAMMO, the Norwegian company which is one of the largest manufactures in Europe.*

They estimated that today the whole of Europe is able to produce about 500,000 rounds of ammunition per year. Meanwhile, Ukraine's demand is about 600,000 round of ammunition per month.

When will the last missile will be fired in Ukraine?

Scott Ritter: The last missile will be fired in Ukraine when the Ukrainian Army is defeated and the Ukrainian government surrenders. Hopefully that's sooner rather than later.

The data you brought out shows just how difficult a situation Ukraine finds itself in, and it also underscores just how impressive the Russian military resources have been. Because Russia is not just fighting Ukraine. Yes, it's the Ukrainian soldiers that are paying the cost in their lives, hundreds of thousands of them, a very tragic loss.

But they've been backed up by the collective economic and military might of the West. Russia is fighting NATO. Russia is fighting the United States. And Russia is winning.

We're getting at the point right now where I think NATO is waking up to the fact that no matter what, not only can they not help themselves get to the position to defend [Ukraine]; NATO committed a strategic error.

I don't know if everybody saw the *U.S. News and World Report* study that came out yesterday (October 30, 2023). For years they do a power structure, power ranking, and for years it's been America, Russia, America, Russia, America. Now, for all of you people who watch American media, you're going to be saying, well, Russia's getting their butts kicked, they're losing a lot of guys, their leadership's incompetent, their defense industry can't produce enough weapons, they can't do this, they can't do that.

Russia just surpassed the United States as the most powerful military in the world. I've been saying it for some time, but that's *U.S. News and World Report*, they've come out and said this. That's a very conservative American [news] outlet. Now, how could Russia possibly become number one, if all that stuff that you're reading about, the demise of the defeat and the incompetence is true?

Because it's not true. Russia has actually become the most competent military force on the planet. They are not perfect. Russia is paying a heavy price, but Russia is winning against the Ukrainian Army, hundreds of thousands strong, that's been backed by hundreds of billions of dollars, the best military technology the West can provide.

And Russia is still beating them.

But it's not just that. Remember Jens Stoltenberg, back in the Vilnius summit (July 2023), talked about the need to create a 300,000-strong rapid response force? Well, they [NATO] can't do it. That's one of the things that this report is saying because if the defense industry can't build the shells necessary for Ukraine, what are they going to do when you build that 300,000-strong response force? What are they going to go to war with? Do they have artillery pieces? Do those artillery pieces need ammunition? Where is that ammo coming from when NATO's gotten rid of all their ammo? So not only can they not supply Ukraine, they can't even supply themselves.

What has Russia been doing meanwhile?

Remember NATO's 300,000-strong response force? Russia has just increased their military from 900,000 to 1.5 million; that's an additional 600,000! And it's done. It's happening. They are formed.

And how are they being equipped? Through the Russian Defense Industry.

Russian Defense Industry is not only supporting a winning effort on the ground against Ukraine, but at the same time they're building up a 600,000 strong military force.

Russia is the number one military in the world today, and it's not just by the size, it's the competence.

Russia has made a lot mistakes, but they've learned so much. They've learned how to mobilize; that necessary 300,000 partial mobilization exposed some flaws, but Russia has fine-tuned that.

Ask Finland how does it feel to have 70,000 new Russian soldiers on their borders? Not too good, does it Finland? Should have thought twice about joining NATO.

And how is NATO going to help you? They can't even build this 300,000-strong response force. NATO's got nothing. They're empty. They're bankrupt. Their economies are collapsing.

The Russian economy is doing all this, and still expanding. The Russian economy is supporting a war, supporting a major military buildup, 600,000 strong.

Let's look at the United States. We had a recruitment goal last year of 60,000 for the United States Army. They are 6,000 short. They can't meet it. And now you have people saying, "The United States needs to increase its conventional military forces," and we are talking about increasing what, 150,000–200,000, and we can't do it. We can't even meet the 60,000, and we are going to 150,000? Russia has just expanded by 600,000. Number one military in the world. That is the reality.

Watch the full interview.

CHAPTER THIRTEEN

"If You Send Them, Russia Will Kill Them"

| April 17, 2023 |

Ukraine war, already with up to 354,000 casualties, likely to last past 2023—U.S. documents

As many as 354,000 Russian and Ukrainian soldiers have been killed or injured in the Ukraine war which is grinding towards a protracted conflict that may last well beyond 2023, according to a trove of purported U.S. intelligence documents posted online.

If authentic, the documents, which look like secret U.S. assessments of the war as well as some U.S. espionage against allies, offer rare insight into Washington's view of one of Europe's deadliest conflicts since World War Two...

According to an assessment collated by the U.S. Defense Intelligence Agency, Russia has suffered 189,500–223,000 total casualties, including 35,500–43,000 killed in action and 154,000–180,000 wounded.

Ukraine has suffered 124,500–131,000 total casualties, including 15,500–17,500 killed in action and 109,000-113,500 wounded in action, according to the document entitled "Russia/Ukraine - Assessed Combat Sustainability and Attrition."

Guy Faulconbridge, *Reuters*, April 12, 2023

Ania K: *Scott, in one of your interviews you've mentioned the ratio, which is 7 to 1, 7 Ukrainians dead to 1 Russian soldier dead.*

I'd like to ask you how many of those 7 Ukrainian soldiers were in fact Ukrainians, and the second thing with this ratio, how this number is going to change within next months?

Scott Ritter: I would say that the vast majority of that 7 are Ukrainians. I can't break it down and be more precise, but I know a lot of emphasis has been placed in some circles about mercenaries fighting on the side of Ukraine. But let's just look at Poland, which I believe there are a lot of Polish mercenaries or, you know, "sheep dipped" soldiers—whatever we call them— fighting. The number of Polish dead though is thousands at the most, not tens of thousands—thousands.

So, if you're talking 270,000-plus dead fighters, and the Polish numbers are in single digit thousands; it's a lot, but it's also not.

I think the Poles are the largest number of foreigners fighting. So, then the numbers taper down from there.

The reality is that the vast majority of the people that are fighting on the battlefield are Ukrainians. A lot of people keep saying, "well there are territorial units, the poorly trained guys." Yes, that's them, too, but remember, Ukraine had a standing army of 260,000 troops before this war began, and these were well-trained, well-equipped troops. Last summer some of the Ukrainian commanders were starting to come out and say that in the elite units they have suffered 80 percent casualties, meaning that out of every 100 men, 80 were either dead or wounded. And to be an "elite" unit, a high-quality unit—remember, NATO-trained the Ukrainian army over the course of eight years. The original Ukrainian army was defeated pretty much in Donbas and rebuilt; it was an eight-year process. So, the troops that were there, that started the war, were very well-trained, and that training came from years of training.

And now, in the middle of combat, these troops have been depleted, they've been replaced with people who don't have the training, so the combat effectiveness goes way down, and you have to understand that it's not just about your ability to be a lethal force, but the lack of training also impacts your ability to be a survivable force, that units that are well trained reduce the risk that they are exposed to on the battlefield by benefit of their training, they know their tactics, they know how to suppress enemy fire, they know how to maneuver.

But when you replace them with troops that don't know this, their exposure to lethal actions from the enemy goes up, which means that an already abysmal casualty rate—as I said, elite units suffered 80 percent casualties by the summer 2022—you're going to suffer even greater casualties because now your combat effectiveness has even dropped further.

And so they keep pouring troops in, and these guys keep dying at extremely high rates, and that's the reality of what we've seen today on the battlefield.

The 7 to 1 ratio right now, remember, it's played out over time, so at the beginning of the war, when the Ukrainians had a better trained army, that ratio was less—you're probably looking at 4 to 1.

I mean, the Russians were still getting the advantage, but as the Ukrainian forces devolve, that kill ratio goes up. So today, even if it's 7 to 1, that's averaged out. Today the kill ratio is probably 10 to 1, based on what's happening right now, and as the Ukrainian capabilities further erode and Russian capabilities increase, that kill ratio can get out of hand.

I think before this war is done, in the final battle of the conflict, you're going to be looking at 20 or 30 to 1 because the Ukrainians will have lost all ability to resist. If you don't have an air defense, you're losing everything.

As your artillery runs out of ammunition—I mean, the biggest killer of Russians right now is Ukrainian artillery—as they run out of ammunition, you lose the ability not only to kill Russians, but to influence Russian actions. And so now the Russians have greater freedom of movement to accumulate their lethality and apply it to the Ukrainians. And so again it's just going to become horribly lopsided, and in the final moments of this conflict, we are going to see death and destruction that is mind-blowing. And again, that's why I get viscerally angry at anybody who says, "we need to continue to support," because this tells me that you don't care about the Ukrainians whatsoever.

You know I am on the Ukrainian hit list, they want to kill me, they accuse me of being their enemy, but I am actually the best friend the people of Ukraine have because I want this war to end, I want to bring an end to the death and destruction, and I want the West to stop propping up Ukrainian men to die on the battlefield when they have no chance—no chance—of success.

There is no chance for Ukraine. None, whatsoever. There's no fantasy driven scenario that you can come up with which will have you defeating the Russians, and yet you're going to prepare for a so-called spring offensive where everything that you have accumulated, in terms of Western-trained, Western-provided military capacity, is going to be sacrificed on a battlefield where the Russians know it's coming.

If you send it, they will kill it.

You know there's an old movie—Field of Dreams—where they say "if you build it, they will come"; Kevin Costner's movie about baseball. Well, this one is the opposite—if you send your troops, the Russians will kill them, that is a guarantee, 100 percent guaranteed.

There's a misperception right now because of the tenacity of the Ukrainian defenses in Bakhmut-Soledar complex, the horrific fighting that's going on there between Wagner and Ukrainian military, which by the way Wagner just said, "We've straight up killed 32,000 Ukrainians in that fight alone." But there are people looking saying, "Oh, the Ukrainians can fight."

Yes, they can fight, but that's deceptive. They are losing that fight, the notion of viable resistance is deceptive, it doesn't exist and it's going to get worse as this war goes on.

Watch the full interview.

CHAPTER FOURTEEN

Chips on the Table

| June 14, 2023 |

Ukraine war: Putin confirms first nuclear weapons moved to Belarus

Russia has already stationed a first batch of tactical nuclear weapons in Belarus, Vladimir Putin says.

Russia's president told a forum they would only be used if Russia's territory or state was threatened.

The U.S. government says there is no indication the Kremlin plans to use nuclear weapons to attack Ukraine.

"We don't see any indications that Russia is preparing to use a nuclear weapon," U.S. Secretary of State Antony Blinken said after Mr. Putin's comments.

Belarus is a key Russian ally and served as a launchpad for Mr. Putin's full-scale invasion of Ukraine in February last year.

Mr. Putin said transferring the tactical nuclear warheads would be completed by the end of the summer.

Answering questions after a speech at the St Petersburg International Economic Forum, Russia's president said the move was about "containment" and to remind anyone "thinking of inflicting a strategic defeat on us."

When asked by the forum's moderator about the possibility of using those weapons, he replied: "Why should we threaten the whole world? I have already said that the use

> *of extreme measures is possible in case there is a danger to Russian statehood."*
>
> *BBC*, June 17, 2023

Ania K: *During a conversation between President Putin and President Lukashenko, Putin confirmed that at the beginning of July, I believe on the 6th or 7th, tactical nuclear weapons will be installed in Belarus. Will the United States install some kind of similar weapons in Ukraine?*

Scott Ritter: Let's start with this, so everybody can just calm down—the United Sates will *never* deploy nuclear weapons on Ukrainian soil. It's not going to happen.

One, to do that the United States would have to enter into a unilateral agreement with Ukraine that will violate its commitment to the NATO nuclear umbrella. It would be an extraordinarily destabilizing thing. Ukraine neither has the infrastructure nor training. There's nothing about Ukraine that allows it to be a responsible recipient of nuclear weapons.

And you have to ask yourself, "Why would you give [nuclear weapons] to Ukraine," because it's not as deterrent—Ukraine is already at war. So basically, it would be the United States saying, "We want to die, we want to commit a suicide, we will do this"; this isn't going to happen. So, everybody should just rest easy, no American nuclear weapons, no NATO nuclear weapons, will ever be deployed on Ukrainian soil—ever—guaranteed. You can take it to the bank and run with it.

Let's get up to what's going on with Belarus. Understand that the United States has a hundred B-61 tactical nuclear weapons deployed in five different locations in Europe and NATO. So the United States already has nuclear weapons deployed on the ground in Europe, and the weapons are allocated for non-nuclear NATO nations. That means, for instance, Germany, in a time of war, Germany has aircraft that have been outfitted with the proper avionics and other support, the pilots are trained so that an American nuclear bomb can be loaded onto a German aircraft, which can then deliver the nuclear weapons in accordance with NATO doctrine.

This makes Germany feel like it's a part of the NATO nuclear enterprise. Italy is the same way, I believe the Netherlands is the same way, I think Belgium might be the same way, Turkey as well.

Russia has complained about this from the very beginning. They say this is inherently destabilizing and it's a blatant violation of the Nuclear Nonproliferation Treaty. But NATO has ignored it.

Now, we have a situation where NATO has bragged about, and Poland and the Baltic States have bragged about, the need to destabilize Belarus to the point where Lukashenko is removed from power. There's been some talk around the border, maybe even if that happens, of military force coming in.

Belarus has entered a strategic alliance with Russia. They now have a unified military. They have a sort of close and unified political system, and to make Belarus secure, it now falls under the Russian nuclear umbrella. The Russian government, Vladimir Putin and the Russian military, have decided that they will deploy a certain number of Russian tactical nuclear weapons on Belarus soil, and these weapons have been dedicated to Belarus delivery systems, SU-25 aircraft and Iskander M surface-to-surface missiles.

The Belarusian military has received these weapons (Su-25 and Iskander missiles), and these weapons have been appropriately modified to handle nuclear weapons. And now the Russians nuclear weapons are there. Like the NATO nuclear weapons for instance, Germany can't just pick up the phone and say, "Give me a B-61 bomb today guys, I'm going to bomb Russia"

It doesn't work that way. NATO has to agree that the nuclear weapons will be released, and the United States has to release the weapon to the Germans, supervise it being loaded on, and then the German plane will go where the United States and NATO tells it to go.

So, the Belarusians can't just wake up one morning and go, "Oh, the hell with Poland, load up five nukes, take Poland out." It isn't going to happen. First of all, Russia controls the nukes, these are Russian nuclear weapons. If Belarus is ever to use these, it will be because something has happened, the West has threatened Belarus, attacked Belarus, threatened its very existence and then, Russia will make a determination, together with Belarus, that nuclear weapons release authority is there, and they will release the weapons, and Belarus will deliver the weapons where the Russians tell them to deliver them.

Having said all of that, the likelihood of these weapons ever being used is slim to none, but it's an inherently destabilizing situation. It's an expansion of nuclear capacity, not a retraction, and I think we all should be in favor of retracting nuclear profiles, nuclear weapon systems, etc.

It's an expansion, but it's an expansion that, frankly speaking, is absolutely necessary if we're ever to be able to get rid of these weapons.

Why? Because the United States has an imbalance in capability, we have a hundred B-61 bombs on European soil allocated to NATO. Russia had no equivalent. So, when you get into horse trading in the nuclear disarmament talks, there is no Russian equivalent for that. So, Russia, when asking the United States to get rid of that [the B-61 bombs], the United States, of course, is saying, "Well, what's in it for us? What do we get out of this?"

And if Russia can't give something that's analogous to it, the United States is going to say, "No, we're going to continue to hold onto this thing."

Now Russia has the analogy, they say we have our nuclear weapons in Belarus, if you want us to get rid of these, then you got to get rid of those.

And now we have created the situation where we can't possibly in the future talk about responsible arm control. It's the same thing that had happened with the INF Treaty. The Russians deployed the SS-20 missile in the 1970s, and NATO had no equivalent to it. Russia had this uniliteral advantage that threatened to destabilize Europe. So, in order to get the Russians or the Soviets to agree to get rid of the SS-20, we had to deploy ground launched cruise missiles and Pershing II missiles into Europe—a very dangerous thing to do—but now that we put chips on the table, we had chips to get rid of, and what happened? We signed the INF Treaty, and all the chips were removed from the table.

So, this isn't necessarily a bad situation. It's unfortunate, it's an escalation, but it does leave the window open for equitable arms control down the road that gets rid of all those nuclear weapons of this nature, the hundred B-61 bombs and the Russian tactical nuclear weapons that have been allocated to Belarus.

Watch the full interview.

CHAPTER FIFTEEN

Politics by Other Means

| August 30, 2022 |

Unreleased Report Finds Faults in Amnesty International's Criticism of Ukraine

The rights group commissioned an independent review of its August accusation that Ukrainian forces illegally put civilians in harm's way.

Amnesty International's board has sat for months on a report critical of the group after it accused Ukrainian forces of illegally endangering civilians while fighting Russia, according to documents and a person familiar with the matter.

The 18-page report, a copy of which was obtained by The New York Times, underscores the complexity of applying international law to aspects of the conflict in Ukraine — and the continuing sensitivity of a matter that prompted a fierce and swift backlash to the human rights group.

In a lengthy statement on Aug. 4, Amnesty International accused Ukrainian forces of a pattern of illegally putting "civilians in harm's way" by housing soldiers nearby and launching attacks from populated areas. Russia, which has shelled civilian buildings and killed many civilians, portrayed the finding as vindication, but it otherwise incited outrage.

Charlie Savage, *The New York Times*, April 27, 2023

Ania K: *What do you think about the words of the Russian Defense Minister, Sergei Shoigu, on August 24th, six months after the start of the SMO in Ukraine, where he announced a deliberate slowdown in its pace. He explained that it was a conscious decision and necessary to minimize civilian casualties. He stressed that SMO is proceeding accordingly to the plan and all the tasks will be completed.*

Do you think Russia will complete the SMO on their own timing, the conflict will end or, because of those "stimulations" coming from Poland and NATO, they will create from that another conflict that will be an actual war?

Scott Ritter: It's a good question. Let's start with just a fundamental, basic principle—war is an extension of politics by other means. And what that means is that war itself does not exist in isolation. A war exists to accomplish objectives, it exists because conditions were met of a non-military nature—usually geopolitical, political or economic—come together, and war becomes a mechanism to resolve these issues, or to create a set of circumstances following the end of the conflict.

So when you say that this war ends, the war doesn't end because the shooting stops. War is a part of a larger process, so at some point the shooting will stop. But the war is being used to shape geopolitical reality by either side. NATO is trying to shape a geopolitical reality that has a weakened Russia at the same time it creates the circumstances for which they can justify the continued expansion of NATO, physically in terms of geography but also in terms of its military—you know, Stoltenberg's infamous 300,000 men.

The Russians are using this conflict not only to resolve the situation in Ukraine, but to create a set of circumstances that makes the Russian vision of a new European security framework viable, to redefine the reality of European security in a way that compels Europe to accept Russia's conditions, the ones that were set forth in December 17th of last year (2021) with the draft treaties they provided the United States and NATO, both of which were dismissed.

When the shooting ends, we're going to have one of two scenarios unfolding. One scenario is a weakened Russia with a strong NATO seeking to assert itself; the other one is weakened NATO with a strong Russia seeking to redefine European security framework. Neither one of those is necessarily conducive to continued conflict.

I actually believe that the Russian scenario is going to be the one that plays out, that Russia is going to win decisively in Ukraine, and that Russia will use this new geopolitical reality to pressure Europe into accepting most, if not all, of Russia's demands regarding a new European security framework. NATO will not be able to respond because NATO is bleeding itself white right now by supporting Ukraine, they're literally draining their arsenals, combining the fact that they are allowing billions of dollars of military resources to flow into Ukraine without a plan or the economic capacity to replace this material.

It would be one thing if the European economy was running on all cylinders. Even then, it would be very difficult, if not impossible, for Europe to reconstitute the military capacity being given to Ukraine in a timely fashion. It would take years to rebuild, and that with the economy functioning. Europe's economy is doing anything but functioning right now, so the idea that this dysfunctional European economy is going to be able to generate a replacement military capacity to replace that which they're sending to Ukraine, at the same time to generate new military capacity to meet Stoltenberg's 300,000 man benchmark, it's a fantasy.

Europe is gutted; it has no military. Europe cannot rebuild its military.

So, at the end of this conflict, you will be looking at a very weak Europe faced off against a very strong Russia, and I don't believe there's going to be a further conflict. Russia is not looking for a conflict. It's Polish fantasy to believe that Russia will seek to move from Ukraine to Poland. Russia has no intention of doing this, it doesn't want to do it, it would be the worst thing Russia could do, because that would trigger Article 5 [of the NATO Charter, calling for collective self-defense].

While Russia may prevail in a large-scale ground conflict with Europe, it isn't going to be easy. It will require general mobilization, it will be extraordinarily disruptive to the Russian economic recovery that's ongoing, both from the pandemic and the sanctions. It would actually lead to the economic collapse of Russia.

And for many of the relationships that Russia has developed with the world which has rejected the western sanctions against Russia, these relationships could become strained if Russia now ends up in a war with NATO. So, it's pure childish fantasy to say, "Oh Russia is going to clean up Ukraine and then make a move on Europe"; they are not.

This is my belief. I don't sit next to Putin or Shoigu, so I don't know what Russians are thinking, but logic and understanding of Russia's history, and just the way that their policies are conceived and implemented, I just don't see that there's a snowball chance in hell that Russia would be seeking to move on to Poland after this conflict. This is a pure fearmongering on the part of Polish politicians, and you hear the same thing coming out of the Baltics, three little puppies, barking, barking, barking. But that's all they've got, there's no real threat, they're barking at nothing.

But most importantly, Europe is not going to be ready to play this game. I think one of the big risks for Poland—let me put on my Polish hat for a second, and I very rarely do this—Poland, wake up! You are by yourself! Europe is not your friend, they don't like you, they probably like you less than Russia likes you. Russia at least understands you. Russia understands the history. Russia is mature enough to have responsible relations with you.

Europe will abandon you at the drop of a hat because you are not Europe—you think you are, but you are not.

Look at how you were interacting with Europe before Russia invaded Ukraine. Were you buddy-buddy or, well, were they talking about kicking you out of the European Union? Come on, Poland, wake up! Are you trying to play this game of pretending there's a threat from Russia, on the hopes that Europe will rally to your support? The only nation that rallies is the United States, and that's not real because the United States can't afford to back up the promises it's made with real military force. So, you're going to find yourself isolated because the rest of Europe is going to be willing to make a new security deal with Russia post-Ukraine conflict, one that seeks to maybe re-establish some economic ties.

I think one of the things that's been proven here is that there's a reason why Europe sought out cheap Russian energy; it was cheap and there was a lot of it, and it helped your economies to thrive. Now you're dealing with the fact that the energy prices are going through the roof, and they're not going to come down anytime soon, and if they do come down it might not be much left for the energy to power up—industries will be shutting down, people are going to lose their jobs, there will be homelessness, there will be people cold, hungry. This is the kind of stuff no one expected to see in Europe in this day and age. You're supposed to be a civilized continent, but Europe is going back to the stone age, partly because of policies promulgated by Poland.

So, Poland, understand that you're slicing your own throat. Cease and desist, stop the nonsense, start looking for an off-ramp. Start building bridges of peace and understanding. Here's another thing, Poland: Do you know who Stepan Bandera was? You know it. You have the monuments to the children his followers slaughtered. They [the Ukrainians] don't view you as humans, you are sub-humans to them. Why are you helping them? It makes no sense.

Now, about slowing down the pace of the SMO. When I read that, the first thing I said was, "Oh, all the war mongers in the West are going to say, see, we're beating the Russians, we forced them to slow down." What they don't understand is at the same time, they're saying that Amnesty International, along with the increasing number of anti-Russian, pro-Western media outlets, have to acknowledge the truth: that Ukraine is using its own population as human shields, extensively. The vast majority of Ukrainian civilians that have been killed in this conflict were killed because their own government uses them as human shields in violation of international humanitarian law, in violation of the law of war.

The other thing I'll point out is one dead civilian is too many, but any time you have conflict in an area like Ukraine—built up—there will be so-called collateral damage, meaning civilians will die.

The United States, Great Britain and Canada, we invaded Normandy in 1944 to liberate France, and I don't think the French resent that at all. But you know we killed 60,000 French civilians in the liberation—the battle for Normandy killed 60,000 French civilians because war is hell, and war is especially hell for civilians caught in between the fighting. Now, when you take a look at the fighting that's going on in Ukraine, and the number of casualties, I mean you had the Ukrainian document released from, leaked from the Ukrainian Ministry of Defense, sometime in late April 2023, that said 191,000 Ukrainian soldiers were casualties. This is before the Ukrainians started suffering their casualties at around 500 a day, so one can safely say that there's 300,000 Ukrainian casualties of whom 80,000–100,000 are dead.

The Russians, I believe, have suffered extensive casualties, I'm thinking in the area of 15,000 dead, including the militias for Donetsk and the Lugansk People's Republic, they're paying a very high price, and maybe another 35,000–40,000 wounded, so we're talking 60,000 Russian casualties. Significant.

When you talk that kind of damage, you should be looking at civilian death count that would be roughly, I'd say 20,000–30,000 dead civilians, would be expected. They're not anywhere close to that. We are talking thousands, but we're talking single digit thousands.

Why? Not because of the Ukrainians—they use them as shields.

Why? Because the Russians have been assiduous in the way they prosecute this conflict. They bend over backwards to save civilian lives. And now we're getting into the stage of the conflict where the Russian assault on these prepared Ukrainian defensive positions is increasingly putting Russian forces in contact with civilians being used by the Ukrainians as human shields. So, the Russians have to slow things down. They have to be very careful in how they target, very careful in how they apply their force, they have to make sure that they're maximizing Ukrainian military casualties while minimizing Ukrainian civilian casualties. That's what Shoigu is doing.

Anybody who has been following the fighting since Shoigu made that statement knows that Russia has not stopped its offensive. In fact, Russia is making significant gains and Russia will continue to make significant gains.

Now we're talking about the Ukrainian counter-offensive, but it's failing spectacularly and Russia will respond to that. The point is that the Russians have done everything humanly possible to minimize civilian casualties.

They're getting no credit for it. They are doing things that no American military leader or American President would be forgiven for doing by the American people. To be frank, when we go to war our number one priority is the preservation of American life, we weren't willing to go street to street Mosul, even though there were tens of thousands of Iraqi civilians trapped in there, to clean out ISIS. No, because Americans would die and we couldn't have Americans dying, so we pulled back and flattened the neighborhoods, killing all the civilians.

But that was okay because there were some ISIS people in there, and that's what we had to do. There's been no condemnation. You don't see anybody in international community raising a red flag about the number of people we killed in Raqqa when we took that over, the Syrian city that ISIS took over as its capital, when we flattened that city. Even in the final days, when we dropped bombs on the final ISIS positions, you had ISIS soldiers hiding among a crowd of women and children, and we dropped a bomb on them, killing them all because there were soldiers there. Nobody cried. Nobody whined. The U.S. military, that's what we do man, those are unfortunate collateral consequences.

You don't see the Russians doing this. The Russians aren't doing this. They're not dropping bombs on civilians. They're not leveling apartments. Look at the battle for Mariupol. If there had been Marines there—I love my Marines—but if we come up to a building and the enemy has fortified it with multiple firing points, we flatten that building, we take it down. "Oh no…there were 60 civilians there?"

Too bad. Life is tough being a civilian in a war zone.

What did the Russians do? They sent their troops forward, getting shot at, to get to the basement, form a corridor to evacuate the civilians, before they assault the building. They lost men rescuing civilians, and it had no military value, none, whatsoever. The military value would have been to sit back and flatten the building and just say "tough luck."

They didn't do that. They lost men. In America, American military commander would be relieved for doing this, fired because he hazarded his troops unnecessarily. We don't give people brownie points for saving civilian lives.

The Russians should issue a medal, just for that. A medal of courage that said: "I committed an act of courage to save human civilian life in a combat environment."

They would be giving those medals out by the handful.

Watch the full interview.

CHAPTER SIXTEEN

Held Hostage

| October 28, 2022 |

Road to war: U.S. struggled to convince allies, and Zelensky, of risk of invasion

According to the intelligence, the Russians would come from the north, on either side of Kyiv. One force would move east of the capital through the Ukrainian city of Chernihiv, while the other would flank Kyiv on the west, pushing southward from Belarus through a natural gap between the "exclusion zone" at the abandoned Chernobyl nuclear plant and surrounding marshland. The attack would happen in the winter so that the hard earth would make the terrain easily passable for tanks. Forming a pincer around the capital, Russian troops planned to seize Kyiv in three to four days. The Spetsnaz, their special forces, would find and remove President Volodymyr Zelensky, killing him if necessary, and install a Kremlin-friendly puppet government.

Separately, Russian forces would come from the east and drive through central Ukraine to the Dnieper River, while troops from Crimea took over the southeastern coast. Those actions could take several weeks, the Russian plans predicted...

On Jan. 12, Burns met in Kyiv with Zelensky and delivered a candid assessment. The intelligence picture had only become clearer that Russia intended to make a lightning strike on Kyiv and decapitate the central government. The United States had also discovered a key piece of battlefield planning: Russia would try to land its forces first at the airport in Hostomel, a suburb of the capital, where the runways could accommodate massive Russian transports carrying troops and weapons. The assault on Kyiv would begin there.

At one point in their conversation, Zelensky asked if he or his family were personally in danger. Burns said Zelensky needed to take his personal security seriously.

Shane Harris, Karen DeYoung, Isabelle Khurshudyan, Ashley Parker, and Liz Sly, *The Washington Post,* August 16, 2022

Ania K: *Let me ask you about Zelensky. One of the guests on your channel said that Zelensky's family is held hostage by the British forces. My intuition told me that he is right. So, let me ask you this, do you really think this really is so, and also how long they will be holding him in this position?*

Scott Ritter: The British Government has provided Zelensky with personal security protection. I can't tell you who is controlling them, I don't know British laws so I don't know if the Special Air Service can provide that kind of direct support, or if it has to be filtered through the Secret Intelligence Service (M16), but what do I know is that for Zelensky and his family, their security is being overseen by trained personnel with extensive experience. In the Special Air Service there are the same people that provide similar personal security service to the Prime Minister and another important British officials.

To say that his family is held hostage—first of all, why are the British taking personal responsibility for it? Is it because Zelensky's life is at risk? Not from the Russians, they're not trying to kill him. You know there's an old saying in the military: When the enemy is doing what you want them to do, just let them do it. And from the Russian perspective, Zelensky is the most destructive presence in the Ukrainian government today. He is destroying relations between the presidency and the military, and straining relations with the West. He's creating economic division internationally. So, from the Russian perspective, why would you kill Zelensky? If you kill Zelensky, then they may replace him with somebody competent, and you don't want that. So, it's not Russia trying to kill this guy, it's different forces in Ukraine that are trying to kill him. That's why the British have taken over, because you can't trust the man's security to Ukrainians, because they may want to kill him.

And now, are the British holding him hostage?

Well, I have to say that when you allow yourself to have that kind of leverage put on you, because now it's the life of his family, and I assume this, there's no reason for me to doubt this, I believe he's deeply in love with his wife and he fears for her safety. I think he adores his children. I think he is a good father. I think he is a good husband. And so his family means a lot to him. And so now, when your family is being protected by this outside service that's connected to a government that's putting pressure on you to do things, how do you tell that government no?

The British aren't so crude, they're not like the Americans. The Americans are just straight up in your face, "We got the dirty pictures of your son and if you don't do what we want you to do, we're going to publish the dirty pictures on Thursday." That's how we operate.

The British are like, "Oh man, that's a complicated situation, I wouldn't want anything to happen to your family, I mean we've got plenty of security there but it's tough, why don't you just help us out?"

Ania K: *So, it's kind of like a good policeman and a bad policeman...*

Scott Ritter: Yes, kind of. Is this literally how they're being held hostage? No, but the effect is the same. Zelensky is not his own man, and nobody could ever be their own man if their family, the security of their family, is in the hands of outsiders who work for a government where goodwill towards you depends on what you do in response to the instructions you've been given by that government.

Watch the full interview.

CHAPTER SEVENTEEN

Politicized Nonsense

| February 16, 2024 |

Zelensky Visits Berlin and Paris to Shore Up Support as U.S. Wavers

The Ukrainian president signed security agreements and sought to push the European leaders to bolster aid as concerns over American funding grow.

President Volodymyr Zelensky of Ukraine made a whirlwind trip through Berlin and Paris on Friday in a bid to shore up European backing at a critical moment in his country's fight against Russia, with support from the United States wavering and Ukraine desperately in need of more arms.

Arriving in Berlin on Friday morning, Mr. Zelensky signed a security agreement with Chancellor Olaf Scholz of Germany that pledged to "strive for a just and lasting peace in Ukraine." The Ukrainian leader then traveled to Paris later Friday to sign a similar accord with President Emmanuel Macron of France, before an expected appearance at the Munich Security Conference on Saturday.

"We are determined to stand by your side and defeat Russia's war of aggression," Mr. Macron said during a news conference on Friday at the Élysée Palace in Paris, adding that he would visit Kyiv by mid-March.

Mr. Scholz said on Friday that Germany would send an additional military aid package of $1.2 billion, and Mr.

> *Macron said that France's military assistance to Ukraine in 2024 would total up to $3.2 billion.*
>
> Erika Solomon and Constant Méheut,
> *The New York Times,* February 16, 2024

Ania K: *Zelensky flew to Berlin. Ukraine signed a pact with Germany. During that visit Ukraine and Germany concluded an agreement on security cooperation. That agreement is valid for ten years and assumes, for example, that in 2024 Germany will allocate 7 billion Euros to support Ukraine. The document priorities areas are bilateral security cooperation, military, political, financial, and humanitarian assistance. An agreement will also come in place with France.*

Scott, your thoughts on this. What's going on? Is this a joke?

Scott Ritter: Well, it is a joke. First of all, 7 billion euros. If I were a German farmer, I'd be furious because the German government has ended farming subsidies so they can divert that money to Ukraine. So, Germany clearly says that we care more about Ukraine than we care about German farmers or the German people.

But 7 billion Euros does not solve any Ukrainian problems. Ukraine has just received a 54-billion-Euro allocation from the European Union. It's spread over three years. I think it's about 18 billion Euro per year. But that doesn't solve anything. Even with this infusion of money, Ukraine is 20 to 30 billion Euros short of what they need to function as a government, and they can't function without the international community putting money on the table because Ukraine's economy is non-functioning.

So, the 7 billion is an absolute joke. There are no security guarantees there, and neither there will be with France. Why? Because both agreements state up front that they need this war to end before they can give those guarantees.

Germany and France know that a security guarantee given to Ukraine now, in a time of war, means that Geramy and France go to war with Russia. And they can't.

It's interesting that Germany is talking about allocating 7 billion Euros to Ukraine during this time. The German defense minister just came out and said, "You know we can't make our 2 percent GDP commitment to NATO because our economy is collapsing. We can't make it."

So, apparently what Donald Trump is saying about NATO not being able to step up, and why America should step up and back them, is a true statement, because the European economy is collapsing around them. German's economy is de-industrializing as we speak. Industries are fleeing or just shutting down because they can't afford to stay in business. The same thing with France. The same thing with England. All of Europe is just going down the toilet bowl of life.

So, they can't make this 2 percent of GDP requirement, but they all sit there, and they insist on committing political and economic suicide by allocating money to Ukraine, which is insufficient to the task. It's not solving the Ukraine problem. Ukraine is a defeated nation as we speak.

While Zelensky went to Berlin, the fortress town of Avdiivka is falling.

The Ukrainians have said the battle is over. "We are trying to retreat but we can't. We're trapped."

Two to four thousand hardcore Nazi Azov soldiers are trapped in Avdiivka, and they can't get them out.

They need to surrender. And when the Russians take this town, it punches a huge hole in the Ukrainian lines, and they don't have troops to fill the gap. They've got nothing, literally.

So, Zelensky is out there in a fantasy world, all about, you know, "Give me aid, I can do this, I can do that."

Meanwhile on the front lines is game, set, match. The Russians are dragging through.

Now, there are a lot of Ukrainians in uniform right now. Zelensky has talked about 880,000 of them last month. Around 50,000 to 60,000 of them have perished last month. So, we're down to close to 800,000. Next month we'll be down to about 750,000; next month after to about 700,000. There are no new troops coming in.

Meanwhile, the Russians are getting stronger at the rate of 30,000 to 40,000 of additional troops every month, because 1,500 Russians are volunteering every day to serve in the Special Military Operation because the Russians are patriotic and Ukrainians are not.

So, what Zelensky is doing, it's a joke. It's a fantasy land. And what Germans are signing up to, again, is just a politicized non-sense. It means nothing.

Watch the full interview.

CHAPTER EIGHTEEN

"No World without Russia"

| February 29, 2024 |

> *Putin Says West Risks Nuclear Conflict if It Intervenes More in Ukraine*
>
> *"We also have weapons that can strike targets on their territory," Mr. Putin said in an annual speech. "Do they not understand this?"*
>
> *President Vladimir V. Putin of Russia said the West faced the prospect of nuclear conflict if it intervened more directly in the war in Ukraine, using an annual speech to the nation on Thursday to escalate his threats against Europe and the United States.*
>
> *Mr. Putin said NATO countries that were helping Ukraine strike Russian territory or might consider sending their own troops "must, in the end, understand" that "all this truly threatens a conflict with the use of nuclear weapons, and therefore the destruction of civilization."*
>
> Anton Troianovski, *The New York Times,*
> February 29, 2024

Ania K: *I have to start with what President of Russia, Vladimir Putin, said today. As we all know, he gave an annual address to the nation. He said these words, which I am absolutely certain you already know, about the nuclear threat: "We also have weapons, they [the West] know it. They know about it. As I just said, we also have weapons that can hit targets on their territory, and they should understand what they are doing, trying to scare* *the whole world. It does risk a conflict with nuclear weapons which means the destruction of civilization. Do they understand this or what?"*

So, Scott, would you like to address these words? There are many other statements, but especially this one.

Scott Ritter: Sure. I think we have to look at it in the context of what happened just prior to this and what's been happening for some time now. Emmanuel Macron, the president of France, convened a meeting in Europe where he floated the notion that individual European nations, including NATO nations, could enter into uniliteral individual security arrangements with Ukraine that would allow for them to deploy their military forces on Ukrainian soil. Not necessarily go to the front line, but to free up Ukrainian forces that are otherwise engaged in rear area security operations and make them available for frontline service.

The situation on the battlefield in Ukraine is dire. They are running out of manpower. They are running out of equipment. We're seeing a collapse of the combat cohesion of the Ukrainian forces.

And so, there's a need for an immediate infusion of troops that Ukraine doesn't otherwise have.

If you recall, when General Zaluzhnyi was being retired—encouraged to resign by Zelensky—one of the big issues that split the two men was the notion of how to rapidly mobilize a half a million men, 500,000 men.

How do you get those numbers in a timeframe that is realistic? And the answer is you don't.

And so Ukraine really has no other option right now. If Ukraine removes these reserves, they create an unstable situation in their rear area that can be exploited by Russian deep reconnaissance groups, create the potential of a Russian incursion towards Kiev, places right now where there are reserves that make this more difficult. These reserves would no longer exist.

So, Macron floated this idea.

But people need to remember that when Vladimir Putin announced the initiation of the Special Military Operation back in February 2022, he straight up said that any NATO intervention in Ukraine will bring about a Russian response that will lead the inevitability of an armed conflict, which will likewise become nuclear in the nature. So, don't think about it.

Well, Macron is obviously thinking about it. There are some fundamental flaws in Macron's thinking, you know. I don't know if he thinks that these nations, even though they deploy unilaterally, that he thinks that, "Will Article 5 [i.e., collective defense] of NATO's charter be invoked if, let's say, France sends French troops to Ukraine based upon a bilateral relationship with Ukraine outside of the framework of NATO? Would Article 5 kick in?"

I mean, what's Macron thinking? We don't know, but it doesn't matter. Article 5 or not, it would be an intervention in Ukraine that creates an existential threat to Russia and would require a Russian nuclear response. And so, Vladimir Putin was putting that marker on the table, reminding everybody that this is real.

He said something else too. It wasn't just about Russia's nuclear capability. He spoke about Russia itself. He said that it's time that the West stopped playing games in Ukraine. You know that there are red lines.

But those games that are being played are designed to achieve the strategic defeat of Russia. NATO and the United States have said this straight up. Jens Stoltenberg [the NATO Secretary General] has said this several times. Lloyd Austin, the Secretary of Defense of the United States, has likewise said that the goal of the United States is the strategic defeat of Russia. And we're using Ukraine as a proxy to accomplish this.

And what Putin is saying is that Russia won't be strategically defeated. It's not going to happen. Russia is a viable nation state—not just a viable nation state, but rather Russia is one of the most important states in the world. Not the most important, but an important member of the global community, that Russian civilization is one of the foundational civilizations of the world, that the Russian nation will have its rightful place in the global hierarchy, and that the West's effort to destroy Russia will not be tolerated, that Russia will defend its rights to exist with the weapons that it possesses, including nuclear weapons.

Putin has once again repeated something he said before, that there cannot be a world without Russia. So, if people are thinking that the world would be a better place if they can somehow strategically defeat Russia, they need to rethink this because the reality is if they ever succeeded in this goal, then the world would end, because there won't be a world without Russia.

Watch the full interview.

CHAPTER NINETEEN

Victors Write the History

| April 29, 2024 |

Ukraine Retreats from Villages on Eastern Front as It Awaits U.S. Aid

Ukraine's top commander said his outgunned troops were facing a dire situation as Russia tried to push its advantage before the first batch of an American military package arrives.

Russian troops have captured or entered around a half-dozen villages on Ukraine's eastern front over the past week, highlighting the deteriorating situation in the region for outgunned and outnumbered Ukrainian forces as they wait for long-needed American military aid.

"The situation at the front has worsened," Gen. Oleksandr Syrsky, Ukraine's top commander, said in a statement on Sunday in which he announced that his troops had retreated from two villages west of Avdiivka, a Ukrainian stronghold in the east that Russia seized earlier this year, and another village further south.

Military experts say Moscow's recent advances reflect its desire to exploit a window of opportunity to press ahead with attacks before the first batch of a new American military aid package arrives in Ukraine to help relieve its troops.

Constant Méheut, *The New York Times,* April 29, 2024

Ania K: *It is said that victors write history, but history is also interpreted depending on the country in which it is taught in such a way that it serves the power of a given country in manipulating society.*

However, let's try to imagine situations where we hope that one day only the true story will be served to everyone in the world. Let's say in 1,000 years, when someone reaches for a history book and opens a chapter on the Russia-Ukraine conflict, what will they read? What will be a short analysis of this conflict and what effect did it have on the world?

Scott Ritter: You're making my brain work too early in the morning. Well, okay, let's play along with this. We're talking about the future so that things can be put into perspective. And to put something in perspective that means that you not only look at the consequences of what has happened, but you also look very much into what led into this conflict. ... [Many will say this conflict] began when Vladimir Putin ordered the Russian military into Ukraine in February 2022. Others will say it began when Vladimir Putin ordered the little green men into Crimea in March and April 2014. Some will say it began in February 2014 when The United States precipitated a coup in Kiev, the Maidan, or what some people call the Revolution of Dignity.

But I don't think it'll be called the Revolution of Dignity because the victors write history. And that term, while it should be put in there, I mean again, I'm somebody who believes that history should be told from all perspectives. And you know that that term should be put in there. So people understand how one party sought to manipulate and twist words to justify their actions. But it wasn't a Revolution of Dignity because no people who are dignified would allow an outside power to come in and manipulate them the way they did. Or allow a political minority to use violence to seize control of the political processes, which, again, happened with the Right Sector, Svoboda, and the other Banderists supporting the Ukrainian political elements.

Other people would say that it began in 2004, 2005 with the color revolution. Again, another American-European Union backed effort to install Ukrainian nationalism at the expense of ethnic Russian elements in the Ukrainian government.

We can keep going backwards. You see, what is happening here is that this war didn't just happen in a vacuum—we keep going backwards to what happened in 1990, 1991 as the Soviet Union began to collapse. What was the American vison? How did we view Ukraine? How was the CIA, which we know was involved in 2014, which we know is involved today, what was the CIA's role in shaping Ukrainian nationalism?

You know, we would suddenly have to realize that the CIA, which stopped officially funding Banderist or nationalist organizations in 1990—when did they begin funding them? Back in 1948? Why '48? What was going on with the CIA—the OSS, actually, at the time—and these nationalists?

· · ·

We'd have to dig deeper and find out the roots of the American intelligence agencies involvement. We'd realize that they were collaborating with Nazi intelligence organizations that used Ukrainian nationalists as proxies. We'd have to delve into the relationship between the Banderist movement and Nazi Germany. We'd have to get into the roots of Banderism in Poland in the 1930s. And we can just keep on going backwards to see how people have been using Ukrainian nationalism for their own ends.

Vladimir Putin spoke about this several times. I mean, famously with Tucker Carlson in his televised interview last February, where over a billion people watched and rolled their eyes in boredom as Putin talked about Ukrainian nationalism being a creation of Austro-Hungarian politicians and generals during World War I to help create unrest in the territories of Galicia that are disputed between the Austro-Hungarian Empire and the Russian

Empire. And we could just keep on going further and further and see how, you know, this thing called Ukrainian nationalism, it's not real Ukrainian nationalism. It's a Galatian nationalism. It has nothing to do with Slavs, *per se,* and everything to do with sort of Greco-Catholic elements that were ethnically, religiously and culturally distinct from what many people call Kievan Rus, you know, the sort of the birthplace of modern-day Russia. And how these nationalists were used, manipulated, turned into this white supremacist group. And I say white supremacist, but everybody was white back then, so it was just supremacist. You know, it was the notion of a superior race separate from everybody else and how it was turned into a cult of violence.

. . .

When people take a look at what this western Ukrainian nationalism stood for and how it dehumanized everybody else that wasn't a western Ukrainian nationalist, I think you will see that there is a psychosis, a sickness that is imbued in this.

You have to be psychotic if you start viewing other people as less than human, and yet this is what western Ukrainian nationalism did.

If you are a Pole, Wolyn means something to you. You know what happened in Wolyn. You know what happened when the western Ukrainians rose up and slaughtered over 110,000 Poles. And this isn't just slaughter...I mean, you know, we are talking about killing.

There is an artist that has painted pictures that are derived from the firsthand testimony of what the western Ukrainians did to the Poles. And I would say that those paintings are not meant for the lighthearted, but when you take a new born infant who is alive and you physically break their hands, break their bones, break their body in front of the mother who you've just disemboweled, but she's left alive, but you've staked her out...and you hack to death people while they're alive, so body parts are lying there...

Meanwhile, to hide the sounds from other villagers, you have a female choir standing outside singing songs to disguise the screams of what's happening inside the building.

And this isn't an isolated event. It happened over and over and over again. 110,000 murdered people. You know this is a sickness, a sickness that has infected certain people. The fanatism of these people has been used by others over history, and that's what we're going to see here is how outside parties have used this psychotic fanaticism that is western Ukrainian nationalism not to further the quote unquote "legitimate Ukrainian aspirations of the Ukrainian people," because nobody has ever respected the legitimate national aspirations of the western Ukrainian people—no one. There's never been an independent Ukraine.

I mean today, we have this entity called Ukraine, but it's not really what the western Ukrainian nationalists want because a huge chunk of this Ukraine are Russians.

Eastern Ukraine was just sort of artificially appended by Lenin and Stalin and Kruschev to create something that could be economically viable as an entity that was never meant to be politically independent from centralized Soviet authority. That's what people need to understand—that when the Soviet Union started expanding Ukraine and creating this thing called Ukraine, it was never meant to be independent. It was always supposed to be part of a larger union of Soviet socialist republics and never intended to be an independent entity.

And yet, when the collapse of the Soviet Union came, the United States sought to use the Ukrainian nationalism to undermine Russia, to help break up Russia, to help weaken Russia, to help ensure that Russia never again could rise from the ashes of the Soviet Union to threaten the West because Russia is still a place with tremendous resources, mineral resources, and as such self-sufficient. The West doesn't like self-sufficient nations because it's hard to bring them under your economic control when they can live without you.

So, we needed to break it up. And we used Ukrainian national-ism to achieve this.

The Ukrainian nationalism isn't, again, a legitimate national aspiration. It is a nationalism defined by Stepan Bandera and the Banderist struggle against Soviet, Polish, and Belarusian rule after World War II. A lot of people don't understand the level of fighting that took place, the violence that took place as these Ukrainian nationalists who used to be allies of Nazi Germany—in fact, their ranks were full of a lot of Nazis.

It's interesting when you dig into history. There was a history that showed the existence of a group, the Gehlen Group, which was an intelligence organization during World War II that oper-ated on the Eastern front exclusively. They had elements within this organization, this group, the Eastern Forces, that would do operations inside the Soviet Union, inside the rear area. So, they would be flown in, or parachuted in, and then they would oper-ate. In, I think, October or November of 1944, after the Russians had kicked the Germans out of a lot that is present day Ukraine, the Germans sent a team in, around 70 guys, and they landed, and their job was to go out and contact Banderists. And they did. They made contact. They reestablished contact. They gave them orders about what they were supposed to do, etc. But when you read the reports, those Germans are talking about how in the Banderist ranks, there were about 700 German soldiers who had been left behind.

You see, when you have millions of Germans running from the Soviets for their lives, many of them go to the ground, go to the woods, and they find common cause with the Banderists. So, there were about 700 German soldiers who weren't able to make it out to Germany who stayed behind to fight with these Banderist organizations. So, the Nazi link is a lot closer than people think. They continued to be directed by the Nazis up until the very end. And when the Gehlen organization was absorbed by the U.S. Army forces in Europe—later by the OSS, and later by the CIA—they still maintained this connectivity. And then the CIA would take Ukrainians from the displaced people's camps in Germany, train them up and parachute them into Ukraine. This is in the late 1940s, the 1950s, to link up with these remaining combat forces. I think the last of them were finally rooted out—I mean, there is some talk about up until 1960 killing individual guys in buildings—but the last organized resistance was in 1954, 1955 when they were all killed.

But then the CIA, instead of saying, "Oops, it's done," the CIA continued to fund this Banderist group in diaspora and have that money and the organizing principles of Banderism put back into the Soviet Union.

When Krushchev came to power, he started this de-Stalinization thing. He gave his secret speech where he criticized Stalin, and he released people from the gulag. He shut down the giant gulag system and got rid of all the political prisoners.

And most of the Banderists, over 200,000 who had been arrested, were released and brought back to Ukraine. And then they began the process of re-insinuating themselves into Ukrainian society and the Ukrainian government, all backed by the CIA.

People don't understand that. The Banderists who came in are being backed by the CIA, backed by the Banderist organizations in diaspora. They made common cause, and they were in the process of insinuating them—to re-insinuate themselves back into Soviet society so much so that in 1990, when the Soviet Union goes away, the CIA went, "Well, look, we've already won, we don't need to continue funding these people, covertly we won, they are in power, we're in power."

Ukraine has always been a CIA exercise, a CIA controlled experiment of destabilizing first Soviet authority and now Russian authority.

This is what history will show when the fighting is done and the smoke is clear and the bodies have been buried and we gain access—the world gains access—to the Ukrainian archives and the Russians finally release their archives.

What we're going to see is that this was a war that was decades in the making; that this is one of the decisive conflicts of modern history. This is a war where Russia has said to the CIA-driven experiment, "No more. You shall not pass. This is it. We are done. We have drawn a red line. You're not going to get away with this. We're finishing this once and for all. This is the end of the CIA's anti-Russian experiment. It's over now. It has failed."

And that experiment includes two other entities, NATO and the European Union. This is all part of the grand scheme done by the United States to control Europe for the purpose of bringing down Russia while retaining control of Europe. And it is collapsing as well. This Ukrainian conflict will go down in history as one of the most decisive defeats of the so-called collective West. It's the beginning of the end.

When people take look at the collapse of the Roman Empire, for instance, a lot of people point to the battle of...and it's skipping my mind...but it's between Atilla the Hun and the Roman Empire. And the point is that that took place almost, I mean centuries before the Roman Empire finally collapsed. But it was Châlons, maybe the battle is...I don't know. But the Roman Empire suffered a major defeat at the hands of the barbarians. And it began, it was a signal of collapse. But the collapse of the Roman Empire began well before that.

This Ukrainian war, I believe, historians are going to put a pin on the map and say, this is the war that signaled the end of the American Empire. That, from this point on, what we're going to see is collapse. We're going to see a decline. We're going to see retreat.

And everything that's going to happen from this point on is all linked to this.

The rise of BRICS as an economic and political counterweight to the U.S. controlled G7, G20. BRICS was accelerated by this conflict. This conflict compelled not only Russia and China to come together to breathe relevance into BRICS, because BRICS predated this by a decade. But up until then nobody really took it seriously. It wasn't a serious organization. What could it do? The G7 was so much more influential. But now Russia and China came together and said, "We must create a counter to the rules-based liberal order, you know the international order that the United States is promoting."

The sanctioning of Russia liberated Russia actually, in many ways. It broke the back of the oligarchs who had seized control of the Russian institutions back in the 1990s and still had control of it. You know, it's funny, everybody talks about Vladimir Putin as this absolute dictator. The truth is he is not, never has been. Vladimir Putin inherited a fundamentally broken country. To keep this country alive, he had to allow a lot of things to happen that under normal circumstances you would never allow to happen. The amount of corruption that has seeped into every aspect of the Russian society. You can't come in and say, "It's all done." You can't come in and say, "It's all finished." What you have to do is to say, "This stink but this stinks more. I'm going to solve this problem. My number one priority is getting pensions for the old people, its creating stability, which means I am going to tolerate a lot of this garbage that's going on right now." And as you build institutions while you're tolerating garbage, the garbage infiltrates the institutions.

You know, I'm not saying [Alexei] Navalny was wrong. Navalny was right when he said that Russia was inherently corrupt. It was, but it's not Putin's fault. That's where he made a mistake, to sit there and say, this is Vladimir Putin's Russia. Vladimir Putin inherited Boris Yeltsin's Russia and is trying to fix it, something you can't do it overnight.

You have to work, and you're being attacked from all fronts. You have the Chechen War. You have to solve the problem in

Chechnya. You have the expansion of NATO. You have a whole bunch of stuff happening which means that you have to maintain a semblance of domestic political order. You can't go around and have a revolution and expect the people to back you while you're being attacked from abroad. So, it's a slow process.

. . .

But when the West sanctioned Russia and then sanctioned the oligarchs, it was the greatest favor for Putin the West could ever do.

He went, "Wait a minute…You just disenfranchised the oligarchs. Thank you. I've been waiting a long time to do that. They're gone."

Now, he could get hard. Now, he turns to the pro-western element of his economy. The West made it easy, too, because Putin couldn't have done the divorce. That would have had the 30 percent of the population—because never forget, Russia is a democracy—and 30 percent of the population would have flipped over to the opposition. He would have lost elections, and he was only winning by 52, 53, 54 percent—he would have lost those elections, so he couldn't unplug, but the West unplugged for him, and he went, "Don't blame me, the West did it," and they [the pro-West element] came to him.

And now, the final thing, he [Putin] just had an election during wartime, again the election that just happened this year, it could not have happened under the similar conditions without the war. What the war did, and again, it's a war that was imposed on Putin who, being a great boxer—reacting, moving, and jabbing, and they put this war on him, and he sits there, and he says, "Wait a minute"—because he wanted this war over, we know he did, that was the design of the conflict. The Special Military Operation was supposed to come in, intimidate Ukraine to the negotiating table, and have this war done within a month or two.

We know this because the Istanbul communique that was ready to be signed on April 1, 2022, would have achieved just that.

So, Putin wasn't using this conflict for some master plan, like NATO accuses him of. He has been forced to react to everything, sustain a conflict, carry out a 300,000-strong mobilization, and transition to a military industrial economic base. All of this wasn't part of the master plan. It was imposed on him. This war could have been over a long time ago, but the West kept infusing money into Ukraine, keeping the war going, forcing Putin to make decisions.

And finally, Putin went, "Wait a minute, look what's happened here." I've heard that Russia, when this war started, and a lot of people don't realize this, I would say the majority of Russians, while not violently opposed to the war, didn't actively support the war. "I didn't think this was required. I didn't understand what was going on today."

You don't hear any of that today. This war is an existential struggle for the survival of Russia in the face of a master plan being driven by the United States and the collective West. You know, Russia must do this. The patriotism level has risen everywhere. And the beautiful thing about war is that when you're asking people to make the ultimate sacrifice, and it's not just the thing the Russians get, this is not just about what's happening on the front lines, it's what's happening on the home front. If you go to the city of Magnitogorsk, in Russia—a big steel city—you see there is a statue of a Russian soldier and a Russian worker raising the sword above them; it's the home front statue, it's basically the thing that says what this is about, the home front where the people that made victory possible, the people that took the steel from the ore from the ground and turned it into steel, forged it into sword, handed it to the soldier. You see the same sword in the hands of Mother Russia, at Stalingrad; the motherland beckons, she is waving them forward holding that sword. You see that sword in the hand of a soldier in Berlin, after they won, he has the sword, he's putting it down, holding the child, you see the same sword. You see the same sword being turned into a plow at the United Nations, the circle is complete. But the Russian people know the importance of the home front, and one thing about the home front, when the home front is mobilized to send the sons, and the fathers, the uncles and the brothers to war, there is no tolerance for corruption, none whatsoever.

Vladimir Putin went, "Thank you very much, West, I'm going to hold an election, and I'm going to get as many people to participate in this election as possible, not because of me, but because they're patriotic Russians. I'm going to make this election about Russia."

And he did. Some 77 percent of population went out and participated in this election. In the last election, in 2020, in the United States, the level of participation in the election had the highest turnout ever. I mean 77 million voted for Trump, 81 million voted for Biden, depending on who is counting. But my point is that was only 66 percent of eligible Americans, and that's considered a good turnout.

Russia got 77 percent of turnout, 88 percent of whom voted for Vladimir Putin. That's called a mandate. He's going to be sworn into office, I think the inauguration is on May 7. And when he gets sworn in, there is already a talk in Russia now of a purge. You see, Vladimir Putin knows that he's 71 years old. Again, Russians know their history, they know what happened at the end of the Soviet Union, when leaders held out until the very end. Brezhnev had lost his mind; he was a babbling idiot by the time he was finished. When Andropov took over, he was fatally ill, even though he wanted to do better, age caught up to him and killed him with cancer. He was replaced by Chernenko, who was literally brain dead when they swore him in, but he was the establishment.

It was only after Chernenko died, that Gorbachev in his 50s became the next leader, but by that time the system had collapsed so much that Gorbachev was unable to save it. And it led to the 1990s, and Boris Yeltsin, who turned into an aged, drunken, ridiculous man by the time he was over. Vadimir Putin stepped in, a man in his 40s, and he became the president. Today he is 71. Okay, he has 6 years, then he'll be 77. Now, he's a young man still, I mean he's active. He's physically active. He speaks very well, but he's not immortal. And come 2030, at the next election, if Russia's still looking to a 77-year-old man for its future, Russia's got problems, and Putin knows this.

But he must fix Russia. He can't allow Russia to continue to be that which he inherited from Boris Yeltsin. The remnants of that diseased regime must be removed. And he's going to remove them. And the war enabled him to do this. So that's another thing about this war. It is transformational. Not only geopolitically on a global scale, but it's also transformational for Russia. The Russia that's going to emerge because of the political decisions of Vladimir Putin is going to make within the next six years could not have happened without this war. Putin's hands were tied. The level of corruption, the level of disease, the level of sickness, that infected Russia was still there.

I mean, I have a lot of friends who are like, "Scott, you're so pro-Russian." So, I'm not pro-Russian. I like Russia, but I am realistic about Russia, I understand Russia, I make an effort to understand Russia, it's a nation seething with corruption— Okay, maybe I wouldn't call it seething with corruption, but it's a nation that has a certain amount of inherent corruption to it. The system of government was inherited from Boris Yeltsin, and Valdimir Putin used it to help Russia survive in these decades, where everybody was trying to destroy it. But Putin was not able to totally purge this corruption from the Russian enterprise. He's now going to do this, and he's going to create a new Russian state that's founded on principles that define Russian nationalism.

And those principles were forged from this conflict. This conflict backfired as far as the West is concerned, because it weakened the West, and it strengthened Russia. Russia now walks into BRICS not the economic weakling that everybody thought.

When BRICS first formed, they're like, it's Russia, but what is Russia? They've got no economy. It's the Chinese, they're going to dominate, the Russians will never go along with it, because you know nobody wants to be subordinated to the Chinese, so it's going to fail.

When Russia sits down at the table with the Chinese today, it's not as a weak cousin. It's a pretty damn strong partner. The partner that has just beat the hell out of the collective West. Now, they did it with Chinese assistance, but Chinese now also understand that they need Russia. They need strong Russia to move forward with the BRICS enterprise. This happened because of this conflict.

Everything the West thought they were trying to achieve, by bringing this conflict to fruition—because remember, this war didn't happen by accident. In 2008 William Burns, the then-U.S. ambassador to Russia, wrote a memorandum called, "Nyet Means Nyet" ("No Means No"), about the danger of NATO trying to bring Ukraine into its ranks. And he, at that time, said, "If we do this, it's a red line that Russia will not tolerate. It will inevitably lead to a conflict with Russia. A war that will have Russia, at the minimum, invading Ukraine, taking control of Crimea and the Donbass."

The West knew that by inviting Ukraine into NATO they were setting in motion events that would lead to armed conflict with Russia. This war was not an accident. This war was done by design to destroy Russia. And it backfired.

History will show that Russia wins this war and Russia emerges as one of the strongest, most cohesive nations in the world after this war. Russia does not plan on being a replacement for the United States, but what can be said for certain is once this conflict is over, Russia will never take the second seat to the United States ever again.

Watch the full interview.

Afterword

Larry Johnson

Over? It ain't over until I say it is.

Sorry.

The voice of John Belushi from the movie, Animal House, was in my head as I finished reading Ania's final chapter.

Ania's interviews with Scott Ritter, since the start of the Special Military Operation in February, 2022, are a contemporary historical record of what will be seen in retrospect as one of the most consequential periods in World History—i.e., the end of Western Hegemony.

So, just because this book has a final chapter, that does not mean the war and its consequences are settled or that Ania is going to disappear into the mist.

The world goes on and so does Ania; with her regular podcast conversations with Scott and other notable personalities. I am not notable, but I am fortunate to get a regular invitation to chat with Ania about the current events shaking the globe.

I am one up on Scott because I have met Ania in person—she interviewed me in the Café of the Metropol Hotel in Moscow on February 25, 2024.

She is not a phony. I met a genuine woman of soul who does not claim special insight into current affairs by virtue of a previous job. But she has an insatiable appetite of curiosity and is not afraid to ask questions or admit she does not know something.

She brings out the best in the person she is interviewing.

If you enjoyed this book, you can get a head start on Ania's next production by tuning into her almost daily podcast. She has her fingers on the world's pulse and knows what questions should be asked today so that we can understand what is likely to happen tomorrow and into the future.

I am writing this as the Ukrainian defensive front in Eastern Ukraine is starting to unravel at a surprising pace. There are many in positions of political leadership in the West and in the newsrooms of legacy media who are surprised and shocked by this development.

If only they had listened to Ania and Scott over the last two years. What is happening to the Ukrainian military is not a surprise; at least not to those who regularly tuned in to Ania's podcasts to hear Scott's analysis of the events of the day.

2024 and 2025 are likely to be more dramatic and action packed than 2023. The Old World Order, crafted by America in the wake of World War II, is crumbling and a new multi-polar world, where Russia and China will exercise tremendous influence, is emerging.

But this new world will not be one designed to serve the needs of Russia and China alone. The Russians and Chinese, having been victims of Western oppression and violence, understand that a new global system that treats every country fairly must be put in place.

You can be assured that Ania will be watching this like a hungry chicken watches a bug.

You can count on that.

Larry Johnson

Follow Larry Johnson on Substack.

About the Authors

Scott Ritter

SCOTT RITTER is a former Marine intelligence officer who served in the former Soviet Union, implementing arms control agreements, and on the staff of General Norman Schwartzkopf during the Gulf War, where he played a critical role in the hunt for Iraqi SCUD missiles. From 1991 until 1998, Mr. Ritter served as a Chief Inspector for the United Nations in Iraq, leading the search for Iraq's proscribed weapons of mass destruction. Mr. Ritter was a vocal critic of the American decision to go to war with Iraq. He resides in Upstate New York, where he writes on issues pertaining to arms control, the Middle East and national security. Scorpion King: America's Suicidal Embrace of Nuclear Weapons from FDR to Trump and Disarmament in the Time of Perestroika are his latest books.

Scott Ritter has testified before a combined Armed Services/ Foreign Affairs hearing of the US Senate, and before the House Foreign Relations and National Security committees. He has testified before a combined Armed Services/ Foreign Affairs hearing of the US Senate, and before the House Foreign Relations and National Security committees. He has spoken to NATO, the

United Nations, the British, Canadian, Italian, French, Iraqi, Japanese and European Parliaments. He has done public speaking engagements at Harvard, MIT, Brown, Dartmouth, Cornell, Yale and Columbia, and dozens of other public and private universities and colleges across the country. He has spoken before the Council on Foreign Affairs, Chatham House and RUSI (in London), and various World Affairs Councils

Ania K

ANIA K is a writer, traveler and truth-seeker. Originally from Poland, she lived in the USA for seventeen years. In 2020 she started her YouTube channel "Through the eyes of" with the intention of seeking the truth and inspiring people to question the mainstream narrative. In the beginning her channel was more focused on the spiritual side of things however the conflict in Ukraine has change its direction. From that moment on she decided to direct the attention to the geopolitical side of events and create the interviews with those guest who are not only the experts in their field but also have the courage and integrity to question the mainstream narrative of the West. Her dream is to build home in one of the BRICS countries and to publish all of her children books in Russia and China. She would love to interview the greatest leaders in this world and ask them those kind of questions that no one has ever tried before. She believes that the truth will set all of us free and we are fighting a spiritual war for the future of children and the humanity.